D1775867

Strategy
and the
Defense
Dilemma

Written under the auspices of the
Center for International Studies,
Princeton University.

A list of other Center publications appears at the back of this book.

Strategy and the Defense Dilemma

Nuclear Policies and Alliance Politics

Gerald Garvey
Princeton University

LexingtonBooks
D.C. Heath and Company
Lexington, Massachusetts
Toronto

Library of Congress Cataloging in Publication Data

Garvey, Gerald, 1935–
    Strategy and the defense dilemma.

    Bibliography: p.
    Includes index.
    1. United States—Military policy.   2. North Atlantic
Treaty Organization—United States.   3. Europe—Defenses.
4. Strategic forces—United States.   5. Deterrence
(Strategy)   6. Asia—Defenses.   I. Title
UA23.G52 1984   355′.0335′73   83–48737
ISBN 0–669–07508–6 (alk. paper)

Published simultaneously in Canada

Printed in the United States of America

International Standard Book Number: 0–669–07508–6

Library of Congress Catalog Card Number: 83–48737

With special thanks to
Cyril E. Black
Frank X. Bradley
Michael N. Danielson
Eugene M. Zuckert
whose support permitted me to
complete this study

Contents

List of Tables

Preface

On May 28, 1983, the editors of *The New York Times* printed a grimly ironic "multiple-choice nuclear war scholastic achievement test" by a British educator, Peter Villiers. The quiz contained questions such as: "If NATO responds by nuclear means to a Russian conventional attack, the Russians will. . . ." The examinee's choices were: "(a) Recognize that their bluff has been called, and retreat. (b) Use nuclear weapons themselves, to the same level as NATO. (c) Attack NATO by every possible means." The approved solution? According to Villiers—and this was the punch line of the article—"There are no answers."

Villiers is both right and wrong. He is right in that the issues of nuclear war and an uncertain peace do not present, under the guise of an Educational Testing Service objective test, easy—let alone clear-cut—answers. Nevertheless, even if there exist no clear-cut answers, at least some more or less broadly discernible lines of strategic approach can be identified. "There are no answers" is itself a wrong answer if it implies that we can indulge ourselves in Diogenes-like despair while refusing to consider the merits of the contending approaches.

Those whose help I will presently acknowledge have convinced me, and I hope to convince the reader, that the United States faces a crisis in its strategic concepts. I do not propose to present a simple formula for dealing with this crisis or to set forth a specific objective force. I count few tanks and number few planes in these pages, and, wherever possible, I avoid use of the acronyms that infest most defense planning documents. My purpose is to outline an approach to U.S. national security problems in the 1980s rather than to formulate a solution or to detail a plan.

The burden of thank yous that I assumed while writing this book comes with an unusual qualifier. Many, if not most, of those who reviewed parts of the manuscript or discussed parts of my thesis disagree with many, if not most, of the findings and conclusions. Still, my intellectual debt is substantial. Those whom I particularly thank for criticism or ideas while absolving them of blame—and even of association—include my colleagues, Professors Cyril Black, Robert Gilpin, Kenneth Oye, Robert Tucker, and Richard Ullman of Princeton University; General Andrew Goodpaster (U.S. Army, retired), Brigadier General David Goodrich (U.S. Air Force), Vice Admiral Robert Kaufman (U.S. Navy, retired), Major General John Pustay (U.S. Air Force), Colonel Michael Wheeler (U.S. Air Force), Major General Richard Yudkin (U.S. Air Force, retired); and Albert Flax, Rick Inderfurth, Shin'ichi

Kitaoka, Michael Krepon, William G. McDonald, Hilliard Paige, Robert Whelan, and Daniel Yankelovich.

Elaine Mack, Betty Lou Trani, and Gail A. Wenrich were diligent and extremely responsive typists.

Most helpful and supportive of all were Frank X. Bradley and Eugene M. Zuckert, whose criticism and encouragement were invaluable and whose good offices and personal support, together with a grant from Martin Marietta Corporation, made it possible for me to complete the manuscript. The effort also was supported, in part, by grants from Princeton University and the World Order Studies Committee of Princeton's Center of International Studies.

July 1983

1 Introduction: The Defense Dilemma

The time has come for a rethinking of U.S. strategic concepts—the concepts that translate U.S. foreign policy into a plan for the deployment of military forces. The United States has been living off of old intellectual capital. It has been relying on strategies and policies that were appropriate in an earlier context, but are no longer helpful. In fact, a basic dilemma has emerged in the field of defense planning, a dilemma—as I will argue presently—of credibility versus affordability. Furthermore, the nation will be unable to escape this dilemma until planners get beyond outmoded concepts of the United States's role in the world and of the nature of the threat to U.S. interests.

U.S. Foreign Policy Concepts

The Cold War suggested a bipolar world order, with a Free World—centered in the so-called Atlantic Community—confronting a monolithic communist bloc. The idea of an Atlantic Community gave rise to NATO as an integrated alliance (with *integrated* referring to the common cultural-political as well as military purposes that supposedly motivate the principal North Atlantic Treaty signatories). With the eventual inclusion of Japan in the circle of political intimates, the Free World community became trilateral (Western Europe, North America, and Northeast Asia). The North Atlantic and the U.S.-Japanese alliances, which together express the solidarity of the trilateral region, are not merely limited agreements to concert military forces. They are viewed as durable ententes, with provisions for continuing consultation to align the members' political destinies. By committing its strategic forces to the security of Europe and Japan, the United States spread the nuclear umbrella over the whole trilateral community. It thereby pledged American cities as hostages to secure the allies from attack.

However, an arrangement that made political and strategic sense in the 1950s seems to make for deepening strategic and political problems in the 1980s. How far can this posture of extended deterrence extend and still remain credible? How long can the United States expect its allies—let alone its enemies—to believe that it will offer itself up to the danger of nuclear war in the name of solidarity?

1

The extended pledge may have remained credible as long as the United States enjoyed overwhelming nuclear superiority. It might have remained credible if the trilateral partners had continued to enjoy such a degree of political intimacy that each member could feel justified in indefinitely sharing the ultimate peril of the whole community (as the one-for-all pledge in Article 5 of the North Atlantic Treaty originally implied). The Soviet Union, however, has long since achieved the ability to devastate the United States in retaliation for a U.S. attack. The United States's nuclear superiority is gone—gone forever—and the driving impulse within the trilateral region today is not the spirit of community. Rather, it is a growing concern for the much-publicized disarray in NATO and for the beggar-thy-neighbor economic policies that the trilateral trading partners are increasingly pursuing. With the passing of nuclear superiority and the waning of the community spirit, the credibility of the U.S. pledge to the allies inevitably has begun to erode.

The credibility of that pledge cannot fail to erode further with the growing awareness that the imagery of community could, in certain instances, involve the United States in a general nuclear war. It is this awareness that evokes images of a holocaust—the second element in U.S. foreign policy imagery that needs to be rethought.

A nuclear war would raise peculiar escalatory pressures and peculiar difficulties of limiting collateral damage to noncombatants—including those ultimate noncombatants, the members of generations yet to be conceived. Understandably, therefore, the reassessment of U.S. defense policy that has been underway since detente broke down in the 1970s centers on a clutch of nuclear-related issues: What is the best way to counter the Soviet strategic threat, or to define a more credible U.S. nuclear policy in Europe, or to end the nuclear arms race, or to prevent the proliferation of nuclear weapons, or to . . . well, cope somehow with the nuclear genie?

Defense planners in the Carter and Reagan administrations adopted a nuclear policy aimed at restoring a power balance that seemed to have tilted against the United Staes. The Carter and Reagan planners tried to cope by conjuring up a bigger, meaner nuclear genie than the Soviet Union had managed to produce.[1] At the other extreme of the nuclear spectrum, a coalition of political leaders, academics, and citizen lobbyists were calling for dramatic reversals in the Carter-Reagan policies. The proposals, centered on the strategic arms race, ranged from the much-debated bilateral freeze on strategic warhead production to grassroots demands for unilateral disarmament.[2]

At a midway position between these extremes, there emerged a group of critics who focused, not on the terror of the strategic arms build up, but on the escalatory potential of theater nuclear weapons (that is, relatively low-yield warheads intended for use in a limited war, particularly one confined to Europe). By the early 1980s, some of the heavyweights of U.S. national security planning—figures such as McGeorge Bundy, Henry Kissinger, and Robert McNamara[3]—had concluded that the United States could cope with theater nuclear weapons only by putting something else in their place.

Bundy, Kissinger, and the others argued that the United States, in concert with its allies, had to undertake a program of major conventional force upgrading. However, a program of upgrading sufficient to permit a major deemphasis of nuclear strategies might be prohibitively expensive, because, unfortunately, those who urge a wholesale conventional build up have focused their concerns on NATO's central front, where the United States and its allies face numerically superior Warsaw Pact ground forces. In accordance with Soviet tactical doctrine, these forces are postured for a massive assault, followed by a blitzkrieg sweep across Western Europe. Ironically, this imagery of the threat—which also happens to be the third anachronistic element in U.S. foreign policy imagery—contradicts rather than supports the case for a conventonal build up.

Since Stalin's days, the view of the Soviet Union as an aggressive and unsubtle parvenu among the world's powers has fostered fears of a modern version of the barbaric invasions. These invasions could take the form of a bolt-from-the-blue armored assault across Western Europe or even a bolt-from-the-blue rocket attack on the United States. It is the first of these imagined threats—the fear of the massed assault against NATO's central front—that undermines the credibility of plans for a beefed-up conventional defense in Europe.

In order to present a credible rampart against a bolt-from-the-blue armored onslaught, NATO's conventional forces would have to be maintained at great strength and instant readiness all along the eastern border of the Federal Republic (West Germany). Halting a massed assault requires an exceedingly high density of firepower. Only two ways of concentrating the requisite firepower are known to contemporary military science: a nuclear response or so elaborate a conventional defense as to be ruinously costly—costly not only in dollar terms but also in terms of strains within NATO (whose members disagree on the desirable line of strategy) and in terms of the diversion that a ground-force build up in Europe would imply for resources needed to post a naval watch on U.S. interests in Asia.

The foregoing overview of the strategic debate of the early 1980s reveals the inner logic of the defense dilemma: A nuclear posture of doubtful credibility, but one supported by the concept of community, leads to calls for conventional upgrading. At the same time, the threat of a bolt from the blue suggests unrealistically costly conventional requirements. There results the dilemma of the 1980s—a dilemma of credibility versus affordability.

Relevant Images, Special Strategies

As long as U.S. planners see bolt-from-the-blue assaults by 'red hordes' as the main military threat in Europe, either they will give prominence to nuclear weapons as the best means of meeting enemy armored forces or they will continue to search for a way to fund the unfundable: a NATO conventional defense able to stop overwhelmingly superior enemy attackers. As long as the United States, inspired by an anachronistic image of an Atlantic Community, extends the strategic umbrella over to the entire NATO area, a war in Europe presents the likeliest way of involving the United States in a nuclear holocaust, particularly if one believes that theater nuclear weapons would have to be used and that escalatory pressures would then become irresistable. If one argues—as I shall argue—that the United States would have no realistic alternative to nuclear initiation in the event of a frontal assault by Warsaw Pact forces, then one must turn to the search for ways to resist nuclear escalatory pressures, that is, to supplant the imagery of holocaust with an imagery of limits.

It also can be argued that the concept of community, especially insofar as it puts the Atlantic alliance at the center of the U.S. world view, leads the United States to scant on its forces in the waters around Asia in an effort to cut resources loose for a conventional build up in Europe. The United States thereby invites instability and adventurism: at best, directly threatening U.S. economic interests from the Persian Gulf to Japan; at worst, indirectly increasing the likelihood that an Asian conflict could escalate to a major war in Europe (the specter that has haunted U.S. planners since Korea) or even to a superpower confrontation. Moreover, because the types of units that are needed in Europe differ from those that are needed in Asia, forces bought for one area would have limited transferability to the other.

What to Do?

No doubt, deterrence of war should remain the aim of U.S. military planning, and a mix of conventional and nuclear weapons should remain in the arsenal. However, the nuclear retaliatory threat that protects the

U.S. home land from attack will not also indefinitely protect NATO Europe. A special strategy is needed to stabilize the central nuclear balance—a special strategy for the security of the American home land. As a corollary, the military posture supporting that special strategy will need to be gradually decoupled from the U.S. allies in the old trilateral community: that is what the *special* in special strategy means.

To go along with the process of decoupling, the United States also needs a special strategy to deter war in Europe—*special* precisely because it would not be dependent, as U.S. strategy in the Atlantic Community has hitherto been dependent, on the strategic nuclear threat. A half-hearted conventional build up in NATO Europe would not restore the waning credibility of the Atlantic partners' defense posture. On the other hand, the major conventional build up that could prove to be politically unsalable to the allies and prohibitively costly to U.S. taxpayers would divert resources that are needed for a major conventional build up in Asia.

In additon, I shall argue, such a build up in the waters around Asia is indeed overdue. In addition to the special strategies needed for homeland security and deterrence on NATO's central front, the United States needs an affordable special strategy to protect its interests from the Persian Gulf to Northeast Asia. These interests range from the prevention of attacks on the Free World's lines of commerce to the prevention of local wars that might get out of hand for want of an adequate U.S. military presence around the Asian rim land.

Because the contradictions of the current U.S. military posture originate in the imagery of U.S. defense planning, a reassessment of U.S. strategies will not go far enough unless it also involves a reassessment of the ordering vision behind U.S. foreign policy. The international situation in the 1980s suggests the need for a new imagery of world order, for a new image of the threat to that order, and for a reevaluation of the means available for protecting U.S. interests against the threat.

2 A Change in Imagery

In the immediate postwar years, American policymakers identified U.S. foreign policy interests with the Rooseveltian vision of world order, as set forth at the 1944 Dumbarton Oaks and Bretton Woods conferences. Politically, the vision of Dumbarton Oaks implied a regime of sovereign states pursuing their respective destinies—not, of course, without conflicts, but with a willingness to resolve disputes by parliamentary means. The United Nations (U.N.) General Assembly would function, in Senator Arthur Vandenberg's oft-quoted metaphor, as a "town meeting of the world." Economically, the designers of the postwar order sought for a permament cure to the protectionism and fragmentation that had afflicted the world's trading systems in the 1920s and 1930s.

During the interwar decades, the economic balkanization of the world into separate yen, sterling, franc, and dollar trading areas had helped to bring on the Depression. To prevent a similar fragmentation of the global economy into single-currency zones or protected regional trading blocs emerged as an important postwar U.S. aim—not just to make the world safe for U.S. corporations but also to promote wider and freer trade patterns for global economic growth. Those with know-how and high technology to sell stood only to gain from free trade. Those with raw resources to sell, and those whose developing economies most needed the foreign exchange that trade could bring, also had a growing stake in the health of an interdependent world economy.

The Liberal Economic Order

The liberal economic order, as envisioned by its proponents, would consist of three complementary parts: a global monetary regime (the Bretton Woods system) featuring high liquidity and easy convertibility of currencies, backed by a strong dollar pegged to a gold standard; a global free-trade regime under the 1947 General Agreement on Tariffs and Trade (GATT), to be improved by subsequent rounds of multinational GATT trade negotiations; and a global development agenda, supported by new international economic institutions such as the World Bank and the U.N. Economic and Social Commission. The global development agenda would include economic reconstruction of the nations that the war left in rubble and economic growth throughout those areas that came to be called the Third World.[1]

Within a worldwide free-trade regime, the operation of the principle of comparative advantage would lead to growing patterns of global interdependence. In a sense, the scheme aimed to increase vulnerabilities for all participants in the international system, because interdependence would make trading partners hostage to each other's (and third parties') acts of disruption. However, the gains to all members of the system would exceed the costs. Interdependent development and global free trade would enable the less developed countries to follow the economic leaders up an economic escalator. The leaders would gradually shuck off functions appropriate to early developmental stages, allowing these functions to be picked up by the followers. (Thus, the former nemesis of U.S. steel makers, the Japanese, have moved toward specialization in high technology, letting the Brazilians and Indians, the South Koreans and Taiwanese rise behind them to capture primacy in steel making.)

But the liberal vision never unfolded in quite the way that its more optimistic proponents expected. In the United Nations, the Soviet veto became an emblem of the apparent failure of global parliamentarism. The envisioned global economy quickly broke in two: a Free World trade zone centered in the United States, and what eventually came to be COMECON—Council of Mutual Economic Assistance—centered in the Soviet Union.

Even within the Free World economy, it became apparent that some adjustments to the tenets of the liberal vision might be in order. To advance the cause of Western European economic growth, the United States actively encouraged the formation of the European Economic Community: the Common Market, eventually joined—despite French misgivings—by Britain. The success of this trading bloc contributed to the European economic miracle, as did the United States's assumption of the main security burden within NATO. Thus, aided by an economic program at odds with the declared purposes of U.S. trade policy (the Common Market, with its regional tariff preferences, affronted the objective of a global free-trade regime) and subsidized by the U.S. nuclear shield, the Europeans recovered with extraordinary speed. Today, their ability to press more assertive and independent policies gives ironic testimony to the success of U.S. efforts at postwar reconstruction.

On the other side of the Atlantic, there developed in support of the Marshall Plan and NATO a remarkable political consensus among traditionally isolationist Americans. It was during this period of confident and generous institution building that members of the U.S. postwar generation adopted the concept of an Atlantic Community, a politically intimate union of nations with shared cultural values and common historical experiences. In time, Japan found a place in the new world view. A caricaturist of the resulting trilateral imagery might have put the Western Europeans, the North Americans, and the Japanese on one continental plate. After all, the real divide in this bipolar world—East versus West; Free World economy versus COMECON— was not geographic, but ideological.

A communist monolith confronted the trilateral community from across the ideological divide. This monolithic bloc embraced all the satellites of Eastern Europe as well as Mao's China. The East-West divide symbolized the one global instability beside which all other potential instabilities (for example, the old European empires, so soon to be in disarray) paled. Western leaders considered that one global instability to be irreparable by diplomatic means. The Cold War originated in this conviction of the impossibility of useful negotiation and of the necessity of mediating the East-West divide by means of military counterbalancing.[2] To maintain the weight of the military counterbalance against Soviet aggression emerged as the critical strategic problem posed by the larger political problem of the ideological divide. Thus, the Cold War tended to translate the most important issues of foreign policy into issues of strategic planning.

The Weight of the Counterbalance

To solve the military problem—the problem of maintaining an effective counterbalance—the United States developed a new technology (the H-bomb) and adopted a new war-waging tactic (retaliation). The U.S. leaders also developed the hyperbolic vocabulary of the H-bomb era, beginning with Secretary of State John Foster Dulles's own contribution, massive retaliation, and including such other staples of strategic discourse as disproportionate destruction and overwhelming damage, balance of terror, and, of course, nuclear holocaust.

For the better part of a generation, the United States relied almost entirely on the nuclear threat to provide the weight of the U.S. contribution to the system of counterbalances. The so-called absolute weapon gave the United States the ability to multiply—indeed, to exponentiate—the destructive power with which it could intimidate the Soviet Union. Everything about the bomb seemed exponential: the chain reaction that produced the explosion; the exponential increases in destructive yields from the World War II blockbusters to A-bombs to H-bombs, which require energies to be measured with order-of-

magnitude prefixes such as kilo or mega; the feared escalation proneness of any nuclear use, threatening an uncontrollable increase in the
level of destruction. The United States could make the nuclear counterbalance just as weighty as the leaders might ever think it had to be.
And there appeared in due course a new strategic theory—the theory
of retaliatory deterrence—to suggest that the U.S. threat would have
to get weightier and weightier indeed.

Resistive versus Retaliatory Strategies

Before Hiroshima, military forces were used mainly to resist opposing
forces: to stop their infantry charges, sink their warships, shoot their
bombers down—war waging by resistance. Atomic warheads in sophisticated delivery vehicles could, however, be used to threaten such
certain damage to the enemy home land, and in such awful proportions,
that the military's offense must dominate any possible defense. A nuclear nation, then, could break the enemy's will by sending forth vehicles of mass destruction to penetrate his home-land defenses, inflicting
unacceptable punishment at the source—war waging by retaliation.
According to Bernard Brodie, the first and most prescient theorist of
the new era, the only intelligent use of nuclear weapons would be to
deter a would-be opponent from ever resorting to the use of force.[3] To
achieve this deterrent aim, Brodie foresaw an almost irresistable shift
from the resistive to the retaliatory war-waging strategy. Military forces
would be used to destroy the enemy's war potential, including its economy and civil society.

The deterrent value of a retaliatory strategy is obvious: The threat
of retaliation should forestall any need to resist by keeping the enemy
from attacking in the first place. However, a resistive strategy also
generates a deterrent effect, because an enemy can be dissuaded from
attacking once he knows that proportionate resistance will be forthcoming and his hostile move will go nowhere. Thus, the retaliatory and
the resistive war-waging strategies generate corresponding deterrent
postures.

Henceforth, military planners can determine to wage war by em-
phasizing either conventional or nuclear weapons. They can employ
either a resistive or a retaliatory strategy. Their doctrines can stress
either war waging or deterrence, while acknowledging that these are
not mutually exclusive categories of military thought. The terror bombings of Hamburg and Tokyo represented efforts not to deter a war but
to win one that had already become total, and to do so not by resisting
the enemy's forces on the field but by inflicting overwhelming destruc-

tion, so as to break his political will. That is, those bombings represented a conventional/retaliatory/war-waging strategy. The onset of nuclear weaponry, however, seemed to tilt force planning decisively toward a new strategic combination: toward the nuclear/retaliatory/ deterrent strategy that would be called massive retaliation.

Massive Retaliation as a General Strategy

After the 'loss of China' in 1949 intensified U.S. concern that Western forces might be outmanned in a land war, the notion of substituting technology for personnel to equalize the balance of forces gained in currency among Western strategists. This line of thinking, encouraged by President Eisenhower's search for a low-cost defense policy, led to Dulles's new general strategy.

Under the new dispensation, the United States would rely on a single set of forces—strategic retaliatory forces, composed of Strategic Air Command (SAC) bombers—and on a single threat of nuclear reprisal to achieve its entire gamut of deterrent objectives. Thus, Dulles saw massive retaliation as a single strategy for three kinds of missions: for primary deterrence, for frontal deterrence, and for local deterrence. Not only would the massive threat deter the feared bolt-from-the-blue Soviet attack on the United States (primary deterrence), but, under the doctrine of strategic coupling, it also would deter the feared Soviet armored rush to overrun NATO Europe (frontal deterrence). In addition, in line with Dulles's determination that the United States should never again be drawn into a bloody, costly Korea-type ground war, the threat "to retaliate massively at times and places of our own choosing"[4] would be relied upon to deter communist probes in remote locales around the Asian rim land (local deterrence). It was this all-purpose aspiration that qualified massive retaliation as a general, rather than a special, strategy.

In order to support this strategy, Dulles planned to build a structure in which the concept of nuclear counterbalancing would have almost physical, mechanistic meaning. If a mechanical system gets thrown out of balance, the equipoise can be restored with counterweights. To ensure against further upsets, those counterweights can be made massive and monolithic. That is what U.S. policymakers tried to do in the 1950s—make the nuclear counterweights against aggression massive, monolithic. The threat of a massive response to even a limited Soviet probe against any area within the United States's extended defense periphery counterposed the full weight of the United States's strategic nuclear forces against the enemy. To confirm the seriousness of the threat, the United States severely deemphasized conventional ground and naval forces to produce the Air-Force-dominant New Look in the U.S. military establishment.[5]

The mechanistic imagery of the system of counterweights even suggested a way to correct the most glaring flaw in that system: the doubtful credibility of the United States's professed willingness to take large reprisals even for small trespasses. By adding to the weight of the retaliatory threat (that is, by raising the destructive potential of the weaponry), the erosion of credibility can—within limits—be offset, thereby restoring the counterbalance. The enemy still might doubt that he would actually be hit with a massive reprisal, but, on the off-chance that he would, the consequences would be so fearful that the risk, even when discounted for the reduction in credibility, should remain great enough to deter a rational decision maker. In theory, doubts about the efficacy of deterrence always can be compensated for by raising the level of terror, that is, by loading more megatonnage onto the scales in the system of counterbalances.

Central Deterrence and Extended Deterrence

Despite the horrors evoked by the thought of the United States's actually using its strategic weapons, there has prevailed something like an absolute consensus on the need to deter any attack on the U.S. home land ("central deterrence"), and an only slightly less solid consensus on the idea that the nuclear retaliatory threat—awful as it is— must play the main role in central deterrence.

But disagreements have regularly been voiced over the proper formula for the deterrence of attacks on overseas areas that are under U.S. protection ("extended deterrence"). Since the late 1950s, when U.S. officials began to retreat from the strategy of massive retaliation, this deterrence formula has contained three ingredients:

1. The threat of a quick, successful conventional response to enemy aggression, backed by
2. The threat of a restrained nuclear attack within the theater of combat, if conventional forces should fail to hold the enemy, further backed by
3. The threat of retaliation by strategic nuclear forces, if events in the theater should continue to deteriorate.

This formula for extended deterrence implies a willingness to forego immediate massive nuclear reprisals in favor of step-by-step vertical escalation. Vertical escalation means that failure at any level of conflict to contain enemy forces could lead to an upping of the combat commitment—if need be, upping it through successively higher levels of conventional and then nuclear counterattack, even to the level of central exchange.

The strategy of flexible response, which ostensibly replaced the strategy of massive retaliation, coordinates the conventional posture (ingredient 1 in the formula for extended deterrence) with the threat of initiating theater nuclear war (ingredient 2). The doctrine of strategic coupling links theater warfare to the strategic retaliatory threat (ingredient 3). In effect, therefore, this doctrine drags massive retaliation back into the premises of extended deterrence, because it warns that the United States might unleash disproportionate destruction against an aggressor who trespasses on its allies' territory, even if that aggressor has not attacked the U.S. home land.

It would be useful to consider the strategy of flexible response and the doctrine of strategic coupling in turns.

Flexible Response

Flexible response emerged in the late 1950s as a reaction against massive retaliation, on the ground that the United States's ability to maintain the credibility of the all-out nuclear threat had reached its limits. In *The Uncertain Trumpet,* General Maxwell Taylor wrote of Dulles's "hope that some military solution would eventually be found to permit lessened dependence upon Massive Retaliation."[6] Dulles hoped to be able to fight limited wars with tactical nuclear weapons.[7] Taylor—also in search of an alternative to massive retaliation, and also a declared proponent of low-yield atomic warheads—called for a general upgrading of conventional forces, while reserving the option of initiating nuclear warfare.

Implicitly, flexible response meant that the United States would respond to local probes (including communist insurgencies and Soviet-abetted "wars of national liberation") with conventional resistance. Special COIN (counterinsurgency) tactics were devised for the elite conventional units, such as the Green Beret commandos, with which the United States would support its allies' capabilities for local defense. Explicitly, flexible response meant that the United States would withdraw Dulles's threat of massive nuclear retaliation as the main deterrent to Soviet frontal aggression and would substitute a mixed threat consisting of possible conventional resistance (ingredient 1), possible use of tactical nuclear weapons (ingredient 2), and possible strategic retaliation (ingredient 3). Whether it would go nuclear, and at what point in the course of a war it would do so, were left as uncertain variables in the U.S. planning equation, so as to complicate the enemy's problem by denying him foreknowledge of U.S. strategic intentions. Taylor's reservation of this element of uncertainty remains a distinctive feature of the strategy of flexible response, which guided the U.S. defense build up of the 1960s under President Kennedy and which, in 1967, became the official NATO strategy for meeting an attack on the central front.[8]

Unfortunately, those conventional forces on which flexible response mainly relies do not come cheap. Flexible response costs—and costs a lot. The shift to flexible response involved movement along the continuum that has underlain U.S. defense policy since Hiroshima, the nature of which Dulles himself well understood. It represented a movement from reliance on relatively inexpensive weapons of vast violence to reliance on a more expensive force structure, but one capable of being used more discriminatingly. Dulles had advanced the general strategy of massive retaliation for the precise purpose of avoiding the expense of a flexible force structure. Dulles referred to budgetary constraints no fewer than eleven times in his speech on massive retaliation, warning that the Soviet Union could draw the United States into costly Korea-type wars ad libitum, threatening the West with "what Lenin called 'practical bankruptcy' " unless the United States came up with a cheap all-purpose deterrent against enemy adverturism, even at the level of local probes.[9]

The economic auguries have hardly improved since Dulles's time. During the quarter of a century since Taylor popularized the concept of flexible response, the entire constellation of U.S. domestic political forces has changed. Those who had previously been effectively disenfranchised—minorities, the poor—have now put major claims on the nation's resources. That these claims in fields such as health care and welfare are called entitlements suggests just how unyielding a component of the nation's spending they have become. The budget debates of the early 1980s suggested that attempts to fund greater defense outlays out of deeper cuts in entitlements spending would quickly reach the limits of political feasibility. Nor did those congressional debates give much evidence as to the likelihood of funding a defense build up by higher taxes. So, notwithstanding the sense of horror that an all-nuclear general strategy such as massive retaliation evokes, a growing sense of economic limits constrains U.S. military planners from reducing nuclear reliance by limitlessly increasing conventional forces.

It is toward increases in just those forces, however, that nuclear fears have persistently driven the United States since the early days of flexible response. These fears have also driven the military toward the adoption of a new general strategy, albeit one less massive than massive retaliation and less flexible than flexible response.

A New General Strategy

Because of escalatory fears fostered by the imagery of holocaust, U.S. decision makers may be self-deterred from using nuclear weapons, except under the most extreme of provocations, that is, first use by the Soviet Union against U.S. cities. Influential figures—Chicago's Cardinal Bernardin for the Catholic Bishops; the foursome of McGeorge Bundy, George Kennan, Robert McNamara, and Gerard Smith; and Richard Ullman—have urged the adoption of a new strategy, based on no first use of nuclear weapons.[10] The call for no first use presents a clear case of nuclear self-deterrence. It is a clear indication of the fear that nuclear initiation in a European ground war could trigger the escalatory sequence that would end up in a missile war between the superpowers.

Those such as McGeorge Bundy, who seek to outlaw nuclear weapons, as well as others such as Henry Kissinger and Congressman Stephen Solarz—and, it seems, just about everyone else—who seek to deemphasize them, want better conventional forces in NATO Europe.[11] The adoption of a no-first-use order of battle would not mean the acceptance of quite so general a general strategy as massive retaliation represents. No first use would rely on conventional forces for local deterrence and frontal deterrence (that is, deterrence of the massed Warsaw Pact frontal assault against NATO), whereas massive retaliation relies on the U.S. Strategic Air Command for local, frontal, and central deterrence. Nevertheless, no first use represents an unmistakable inclination toward the acceptance of a general strategy rather than a set of special strategies, because no first use clearly favors reliance on a single type of force—a large conventional force—when dealing with a wide range of contingencies: local wars and frontal wars, guerrilla conflicts and bolt-from-the-blue attacks, wars in Europe as well as wars in Asia.

In theory, if those large conventional forces were really large enough, then the NATO allies could stop a frontal assault without evoking the threat of nuclear holocaust. The world could return to the good old ways of civilized warfare—the ways that Bernard Brodie supposed were irrecoverably outmoded by the absolute weapon.

But how large—and how costly—would an adequate conventional force have to be? A 1980 U.S. Office of Management and Budget report suggested that more than $100 billion might have to be spent over eight years to field some eleven new "armored division equivalents" in order for combined NATO ground forces to have a high-confidence defense posture on the central front. $100 billion![12] Unfortunately, Bundy and the others do not mention how the country is going to raise that kind of money at a time when it also is trying to cut deficits, upgrade school systems and roadways, and maintain a social safety net for the poorest of its citizens.

If the United States cannot fund the program by itself, what are the prospects that the cost burden would be shared by all the Atlantic partners? Will U.S. allies join in sustaining the program of conventional upgrading that no first use would require? That is unlikely: For years, the setting of NATO conventional force goals has been an exercise in wishful thinking. The British and Germans have long since repudiated the 3 percent annual increases in defense outlays that the NATO ministers pledged in 1978. At the other extreme of the trilateral region, Japanese military outlays of one percent of gross national product compared with U.S. commitments in the 5 to 7 percent range, speak for themselves.

And so the strategists come full circle: The sharpness of the economic horn of the defense dilemma sooner or later drives U.S. planners to look again at the cheaper—if riskier and less credible—nuclear option. After all, it is unclear why an overseas interest that might merit substantial outlays for conventional defenses would not, alternatively, justify the risk of a cheaper nuclear posture instead. A consideration of this alternative leads to the difficult question: Must the United States purchase affordability—by continuing to rely on a nuclear posture— at the cost of credibility? Alas, this seems to be the case if the United States insists that its nuclear posture in Europe continue to imply strategic coupling.

Strategic Coupling

How can an overseas interest simultaneously be so small that it deserves only a perhaps indecisive conventional effort to defend it (which is what no first use would really end up providing) and yet so big that it merits shielding with strategic nuclear forces? This is the situation that has, in fact, emerged in Europe.

The doctrine of strategic coupling anchors extended deterrence in Europe with the ultimate nuclear threat, a threat that could bring holocaust on the United States as a result of its defense of allies. To ask how long American policymakers can continue to offer American cities as hostages to secure the allies from attack is to suggest the absurdity of the United States's perpetual assumption of the ultimate nuclear risk on the allies' behalf. The coupled relationship made sense for a while, perhaps, while the United States's historic partners (Britain and France) and prospective allies (West Germany and Japan) recovered from World War II. But does it make sense indefinitely?

If the United States's underlying political commitment to NATO Europe could reasonably be expected to hold up indefinitely, then its willingness to endure the ultimate military risk on the Europeans' behalf might hold up indefinitely as well, particularly in view of the fact that the theory of counterbalancing supports continued coupling. Coupling adds to the weight of the threat with which the United States counterbalances the pressure that Warsaw Pact forces exert on the NATO central front; the decreased likelihood that the Soviet Union will start a war—a consequence of the weightiness of the counterbalance—more than compensates for the increased peril to the United States, and hence the reduced credibility, that the coupled relationship implies.

The whole rigamarole depends, however, on the maintenance of some threshold of confidence in the U.S. pledge to weigh into a European war with central retaliatory forces. As the strategic implications of the U.S. gesture to the allies become more clear—if the United States strikes, the Soviet Union surely will strike back at it as well as at the Europeans—and as the depth of the United States's Atlantic loyalty becomes more doubtful, the credibility of that pledge begins to wane.

In this light, the trouble with the NATO dialogue of the 1980s becomes clear. Some U.S. policymakers—and not a few Europeans— seem bent above all on maintaining the unity of the alliance. Once this political objective has been put at the top of the agenda, all decisions on force structure and weapons deployments must support the U.S. pledge to weigh into a European war, even at the risk of ultimate destruction. Anything less, argue the purveyors of the standard view, will exacerbate the forces of political disarray in NATO Europe, thereby making U.S. allies vulnerable to Soviet intimidation and manipulation.

However, the purveyors of the standard view have it the wrong way around. A political objective such as alliance solidarity either must express a genuine political sentiment—that is, a sentiment of real community—or else it must gradually recede from importance as an objective of U.S. national policy. That political objective cannot be put on a military life-support system called strategic coupling indefinitely. Rather, strategic coupling can be justified only if it is a means to achieve a political objective of a higher order.

That political objective, however, already has shown moribund symptoms as a consequence of the political disarray in NATO. Nor is the waning of the concept of community an exclusively European malaise. The decisive form of political disarray—which is probably beyond palliation by reassertions of a U.S. strategic commitment—has already begun to set in. What is more, its onset is to be found among the so-called successor generation of U.S. citizens as well as among some

Europeans. That is why the proponents of the standard view have it wrong when they urge the United States to do whatever it must (at any cost, win the bidding war with the Soviet Union in the Geneva arms control negotiations) to buy another few years of loyalty from the Europeans. It is true that British laborites, Dutch pacifists, French and Greek nationalists, German youth, and any number of other European constituencies make for big question marks in the future of NATO. However, the real job of U.S. statecraft today is not to buy continued European support for an Atlantic Community. Rather, it is to recognize that U.S. interests will not long remain identified with the imagery of community and then to adjust the U.S. military posture accordingly. Irrespective of European doubts about the Atlantic alliance, it is the waning loyalty of U.S. citizens that inevitably bodes the undermining of the strategic logic of the U.S. posture in Europe. It is the waning American loyalty that eventually will force a process of strategic decoupling.

The Erosion of Community

The concept of a community came naturally to the original North Atlantic Treaty signatories—a group that did not, incidentally, include the West Germans, who had never been a westward-looking people. The original NATO partners shared the cultural and historical values that pundits such as Walter Lippmann put at the center of the Atlantic idea.[13] However, at every turn, in the United States one sees demographic and educational processes at work that erode the cultural-historical base of the NATO commitment. The shift of the U.S. population southward and westward implies corresponding changes in foreign policy preoccupations, more toward Latin America and the Pacific. The political ascent of minority groups (Blacks, Hispanics, Orientals) whose roots lie other than in NATO Europe attenuates the emotional appeal of the Atlantic idea. In addition, there is the displacement of the European literary tradition from the center of higher learning in the United States—displaced in favor of curricula that are built increasingly around computer lore, the social sciences, and non-Western languages. The rise of the successor generation also has had its effect on the depth of the U.S. commitment to NATO.[14] It gets harder and harder to sentimentalize the European connection for the younger U.S. citizens who never got in the habit of reading Walter Lippmann and who never thrilled to radio reports of Eisenhower's crusade or the Berlin airlift.

The mystique of the Atlantic Community emerged from the common travails of two world wars. The mystique did not, however, necessarily represent a coming together of the United States and Europe in perpetual political intimacy. Indeed, a waning commitment to the Atlantic Community must be regarded as a perfectly natural development for citizens of an island-nation. As that development matures, it cannot but undermine the strategic logic of the early NATO commitment.

What the United States really is experiencing is a gradual inflection of the U.S. spirit, a return to a deeper pattern of political loyalties. Beneath the commitment to community of the Cold War years there persisted a residual sentiment of political insularity—not in the sense of isolationism, but in the sense of independent definition of national interests. Over the longer reach of U.S. history, the Jeffersonian-Washingtonian concepts possessed the American political imagination—the idea of an island-nation averse to entangling alliances and bent on an independent course in world affairs. Political independence, confirmed by the geography of oceanic separation, would let the United States prosper unhindered by European feudal traditions, by European decadence.[15] The time may have come to return to the Jeffersonian tradition. By comparison with the commitment to community the residual sentiment of insularity represents the more constant substratum of U.S. foreign policy—more constant in terms of the nation's past, and probably more pertinent in terms of the nation's future interests.

What is more, as the cultural-historical basis of the Atlantic commitment has attenuated, the economic factors bearing on the United States's global role have redefined the zone of overseas concern in a way that calls for foreign policymaking under the inspiration of—for want of a better term—a geoeconomic imagination.

A Geoeconomic Imagination

By moving to realign its defense posture with its commercial interests— which would be tantamount to deemphasizing the European connection in favor of Asian relationships—the United States also would be reemphasizing the economic preoccupations that have held a place second only to political independence on the scale of national values.

The Traditional American Economic Preoccupation

U.S. citizens have always recognized that their civil and political liberties depend on a base of material prosperity. The creation of institutions to promote economic growth—to release the productive energies of entrepreneurs—dominated the U.S. political agenda before the Civil War.[16] The same preoccupation revealed itself in the late nineteenth-century effort to industrialize the East and exploit the resources of the West. Franklin Roosevelt's belief that "necessitous men are not free men" underlay the theory of the New Deal.[17]

The same economic theme underlies the liberal vision in U.S. foreign policy, but in an internationalized form. Not even the bounty of the continent, which for so many years sufficed to make the nation a "people of penty," can support a prosperous United States in the interdependent world of the 1980s.[18] Today, the U.S. economic frontiers extend far beyond the country's shorelines. Statistics on the correlations between U.S. jobs and foreign economic growth have become all too familiar: up to 40 percent of the U.S. agricultural product and 20 percent of its manufacturing go into exports. By some estimates, every billion dollars of new export trade eventually takes 40,000 U.S. citizens off of the unemployment rolls.[19] Obversely, every brick added to U.S. trading partners' tariff walls costs jobs in the United States, and every point added to U.S. tariff rates takes money out of the pockets of U.S. consumers by inflating domestic prices. Increasingly, the nation's overseas concern must be focused on its economic outreach—on U.S. foreign markets and resource suppliers—rather than on an ideological contest.

U.S. Economic Outreach

It is noteworthy that the Europeans no longer occupy a special position in the U.S. economic outreach—certainly, nothing like the dominant trading position that was envisioned for them during the years of the Marshall Plan. By 1980, Japan accounted for twice the dollar value of exports from the United States that West Germany did and almost three times the value of U.S. imports. U.S. imports from the Western Pacific economic archipelago (including Japan, Taiwan, and the Southeast Asian trading centers) exceeded imports from the European Economic Community by almost 33 percent. The export balance tilted toward Europe, but by a much smaller margin (20 percent). When Middle Eastern figures—mostly Persian Gulf data—are included in the accounts of U.S. Asian trade, the United States's European trading partners show up as minority entries on both the import and export sides of the ledger.[20] All in all, the country's Asian-oriented economic interests seem difficult to square with its defense policy, under which fully 54 percent of U.S. overseas security expenditures are dedicated to the European theater.[21]

In addition to the changes that have occurred since the 1950s in the U.S. patterns of overseas dependency, significant changes have occurred in trade patterns among U.S. trading partners around the world. Those Mercedes cars from Germany and those Toyotas from Japan come from factories that are powered by Persian Gulf oil. The concept of interdependency means that the countries of Western Europe, an unstable Persian Gulf, the giant developing markets of India and China, and a potential global growth pole in the Western Pacific should be viewed as a single trading zone—a zone whose economic revitalization is essential for a renewal of the liberal vision as well as for a recharging of the United States's own economic batteries. Significantly, two of the most powerful U.S. trading partners in this zone, West Germany and Japan, also have the most tenuous affinities to the Atlantic Community. Their growing importance can serve as a metaphor for the recession of cultural-historical factors, relative to economic factors, in the constellation of U.S. overseas interests.

As has already been suggested, the increasing importance of the economic outreach on which U.S. prosperity depends points to a concept of world order that is rooted in a geoeconomic imagination, rather than in the cultural or ideological concerns of the bipolar era. The *geo* in geoeconomic points to the fact that geography indeed counts, both in foreign policy and in defense policy: the geography of raw resource deposits (oil from Arabia as well as from Alaska); the configuration of land masses and waters (badly strained sea lines of supply around Southeast Asia); the locations of possible military flash points (the U.S. emphasis has been on Europe, while its wars have been in Korea and Vietnam); and the global disposition of U.S. markets (U.S. exports to West Germany, the Middle East, and the trio of Hong Kong, South Korea, and Taiwan account for roughly equal shares of U.S. exports while imports from the latter two groupings not only exceed those from West Germany but almost match U.S. imports from all European Economic Community nations combined).

It comes to this: with respect to the economic outreach defined by its overseas markets, the United States should be viewed, not primarily as the senior member of an integrated cultural-historical community, but rather as an independent island-nation with far-flung mercantile interests throughout the old arc of containment around the Eurasian rim land. Such a change in U.S. world order imagery would promote not only a line of foreign policy more in keeping with the realities but also a line of defense policy more suited to meeting the Soviet military threat.

3 Meeting the Soviet Threat

To complement a change in the U.S. concept of world order—from an ideological definition of the security problem to a geoeconomic definition of U.S. overseas interests—the bolt-from-the-blue imagery of the Soviet threat that has dominated much of U.S. strategic thought must be revised. To see just why and how the United States should change its concept of the threat, it would be useful to trace the changing emphases of Soviet military force planning since the early 1960s and the evolving political strategy of Kremlin leaders over the years of the military build up.

The Changing Military Posture

A xenophobic tradition combined with a persisting imperial urge sets the security agenda of the Soviet Union. Top priority on the Soviet agenda goes to central deterrence—deterrence of the preemptive attack that, Party theoreticians have long contended, U.S. businessmen may one day compel their military toadies to launch in a desperate effort to save a bankrupt political-economic system. A Soviet Union that has been rendered secure from central attack—or, anyway, that has been organized to ensure its survival as a nation even after a central war—can then pursue the second objective on the security agenda: cautious pressing of the communist cause around the world and especially in the areas that border the Soviet Union.

In pursuit of these goals, the Soviet Union has mounted its own triad of bombers, submarine-launchable missiles, and—preponderantly—land-based strategic rocket forces, complemented by a formidable array of frontal forces. A huge, heavily armored conscript army backed by a large tactical air arm can be used in a wide range of missions: to police the Soviet empire (as in Czechoslovakia in 1968); in acts of overt aggression (as in the Afghan invasion of 1980); and for local border security (as along the boundary with China).

The Strategic Posture

In the course of the well-publicized strategic build up that began after the 1962 Cuban Missile Crisis, the Soviet Union has complemented its strategic rocket forces with large-scale air defense and civil defense programs. The Soviet Union not only has enough military force to deter a U.S. attack by threatening retaliation against the United States but also—according to some Kremlin watchers—has the right kinds of forces to start a war.[1] It could launch a first strike that would partially disarm the United States and have adequate defenses to ride out the retaliation that any surviving U.S. forces could inflict. According to this theory, the Soviet Union need not fear being faced down even in the ultimate nuclear confrontation. Because of its defensive preparations, and because the dialectic of history promises it an ultimate triumph, the Soviet Union can wage a general nuclear war and survive—even win. So, at least, goes one claim of Marxist-Leninist strategic doctrine.

During the later years of the Brezhnev regime, Party officials expressed doubts that anyone could win a central war.[2] However, the residual effect of Soviet nuclear war-waging doctrines could persuade Kremlin leaders, in a crisis, to test their theories by actually launching a strategic attack against the United States. Those who believe that the Soviet Union has irretrievably malign intentions, and that the United States has a window of vulnerability, fear a calculated bolt-from-the-blue strike. The holders of this view, however, represent a minority among U.S. strategic thinkers.

More credible than the threat of a true bolt-from-the-blue strike is the threat of an attack on the United States following a superpower crisis in which the Soviets fear such a deterioration of their position that the Kremlin leadership would seriously consider a desperate raising of the stakes. It is in such circumstances that belief in the efficacy of a costly defensive apparatus could make the margin of difference for Soviet advocates of escalation.

The circumstances in which the Kremlin leadership might consider such a dramatic escalatory move brings up the possibility of a European war that turns against the Soviet Union, thereby threatening the Party with a humiliating defeat. This possibility, not community sentiment, is the real reason why the United States must never cease to put deterrence at the top of its priorities for NATO Europe.

The Frontal Forces

Since the creation of the Atlantic alliance, NATO planners have thought of a European war in terms of a bolt-from-the-blue armored attack on the central front. This scenario, however, like that of the preemptive attack against the U.S. home land, has become less credible over time. And, like the bolt-from-the-blue central strike, the bolt-from-the-blue armored attack seems likeliest to come not as the dramatic move by which the Soviet Union would start a war but as an escalatory move calculated to retrieve a situation that has already turned against it. The scenario that the Soviet Union has feared over all others since the late 1940s, and for which it has prepared its forces in Eastern Europe, is the scenario of the U.S. attack against "Mother Russia."

Actually, the credibility of the bolt-from-the-blue Warsaw Pact armored attack is a kind of vestige from the 1940s and 1950s, when the offensive orientation of the Red Army in Eastern Europe supported the Soviet central deterrent mission. The United States held a virtual nuclear monopoly. The Soviet Union, having no effective central deterrent, could not hit U.S. cities in retaliation for attacks on Soviet cities. But it could retaliate indirectly. It could rush to the Atlantic, taking Bonn, Paris, and Rotterdam along the way. Brave talk from U.S. strategists about "decapitating the enemy" by "nuking the Politburo" in the Kremlin might start to sound less brave if the Politburo moved into the Louvre or the Cathedral of Notre Dame.[3]

The use of frontal forces as an indirect threat against the United States has become less relevant now that the Soviet Union can retaliate across the North Pole. Its ability to hold Western Europe hostage, however, adds an important redundancy to the Soviet Union's central deterrent. Thus, the frontal forces serve as a collateral deterrent.

Warsaw Pact units should not be seen simply as a war machine poised to conquer the countries west of the Oder-Niesse line—that is, as a war machine poised for the bolt-from-the-blue assault on NATO's central front, followed by a blitzkrieg rush across Europe. What Western planners fear as the vehicle of sudden frontal aggression also could be used as a lever against the United States in the event of a conflict anywhere on the periphery. In the event, say, of a border incident with China that might bring the United States into military collusion with the Peoples' Republic, the Soviet Union could up the ante by moving against territories that its frontal forces hold hostage elsewhere. Thus, the frontal forces—not the strategic rocket forces—probably represent the most threatening vehicle of escalation from a local conflict. The blitzkrieg moves for which these forces are postured, and their positioning on the margins of Western Europe and the Middle East, could make them effective instruments for the seizure of territories that the Soviet Union would then use when bargaining for an end to hostilities. The point is: The most likely circumstance for military use of the frontal forces is not one of sudden aggression, but one of rising tension as an initially limited conflict begins to turn against the Soviet Union and casts doubt on the viability of the communist political regime.

To appreciate the real Soviet order of battle requires looking still further—beyond the frontal forces taken by themselves. Although the frontal forces continue to pose the threat of major invasions, it is in combination with the new Soviet navy that the main use—an essentially political use—of the frontal forces becomes evident. Indeed, the decisive cue that a new concept of threat is needed comes from the investments that the almost landlocked Soviet Union has made in sea power.

The Naval Forces

The primary naval mission is to deny the U.S. fleet command of the seas throughout the approaches to the Eurasian land mass.[4] This mission requires a major presence on the oceans that also happen to carry the world's most critical maritime traffic: the North Atlantic and around the arc from the Indian Ocean through the Strait of Malacca to the Western Pacific—the Asian Main.

Of special concern to the Scandinavians and the Japanese is the Soviet Union's extension of the effective operating area of its northern fleet to a line from the Denmark Strait (between Greenland and Iceland) to the Jutland peninsula and its extension of the eastern fleet's presence to the north of Japan, especially at the new Petropavlovsk naval base on the Kamchatka peninsula, as well as to the south by taking full advantage of the base at Cam Ranh Bay that their Vietnamese clients have provided. Finally, the acquisition of facilities at the South Yemenese port of Al Ghaida and island of Socorta has extended the Soviet naval presence into the area of the Gulf of Aden and the Indian Ocean.

What hath Admiral Sergei Gorschkov, the architect of the postwar Soviet navy, wrought? By the mid-1970s, he had built a first-rate ship-sinking fleet of cruisers and attack submarines (as opposed to the U.S. battle fleets, which are built around Forrestal- and Nimitz-class carriers). In the design and deployment of Gorschkov's navy lies the potential for the Soviet fleet to put much of the international economic outreach of the United States and its Free World trading partners at risk.

In combination, the frontal and naval forces of the Soviet Union add up to an impressive capability, not only to fight local and theater wars, but also to emanate power in support of foreign policy goals, particularly the goal of influence expansion in the areas surrounding the Soviet Union.[5] Such expansion is consistent with the official Soviet theory of global change—the theory of the changing correlation, which also provides a framework for interpreting Soviet intentions on the international stage.

The Evolving Political Strategy

According to Party theoreticians, the rise of the Soviet state to super-power status allegedly shows that the correlation of world forces has tilted to the advantage of "the state of the people and the world": as the Soviet Union goes, so eventually will go everyone else.[6]

Inexorable historical processes drive the changing correlation. These processes will never cease to generate instabilities within the capitalist camp. The imperialists will continue to make war on one another, as they did in 1914 and 1939; the colonial empires will continue to break up. Local instabilities—in Asia, in Africa and the Middle East, and almost everywhere else—will keep showing up as the forces of change grind forward. Given the Soviet Union's belief that these forces are foreordained to work to the long-term advantage of the communist camp, a prime aim of Soviet foreign policy is to encourage the changing correlation by all means short of major war. To this end, during the late 1950s, Khrushchev broached, and his successor Brezhnev elaborated on, the notion of competitive coexistence as a scheme to advance the changing correlation of forces.[7]

Competitive Coexistence

Opportunistic mischief making, instead of central confrontation with the United States, could be used to abet the forces of dialectical materialism. Avoid central war and deemphasize frontal assaults, especially in Europe, while competing ideologically and—if need be—militarily throughout the arc of developing countries. Under the strategic concept of a collateral use of Warsaw Pact frontal forces to seize territorial bargaining chips, war in Europe could still arise out of a deteriorating local situation elsewhere. Soviet doctrine does not even rule out escalation to the level of central war, either by a direct jump to a superpower exchange or, more likely, through the intermediate step of moving the frontal forces into additional theaters around the Eurasian rim land. However, all scenarios for extension or escalation of a conflict will most likely originate in local wars that erupt from the processes of competitive coexistence. Those processes go forward globally, but they go forward most intensely in a zone of intersecting U.S.-Soviet interests around the Eurasian rim land. (Geography counts as much in a proper assessment of the threat as it does in a proper assessment of U.S. overseas interests.)

The Soviet Union's Rim-land Agenda

The Soviet involvements in Poland and Afghanistan, and the renewed effort to normalize relations with the Peoples' Republic of China, may be regarded as elements in a continuing effort to buffer Soviet borders against military attack and to proof them against imported sources of political unrest. Centuries of vulnerability to invasion from Europe and central Asia helps to explain the Soviet Union's preoccupation with boundary security. Hence, the Soviet Union has persistently resisted any course of events that could lead to a reunited, remilitarized Germany. Historical vulnerability also helps to explain the Soviet Union's concern over the spread of Islamic nationalist unrest on its borders in the Middle East. And, of course, the invasion proneness of the Russian home land from the East, going back to the Mongols, helps to explain Soviet fears of a more radically hostile foreign policy by the Chinese.

George Kennan once remarked on the Soviet habit of confusing the offense with the defense.[8] The communists, like the czars before them, have tried to control the historic avenues of military invasion or political infection mainly by means of expansion around the perimeter of the Soviet state, thus serving an essentially defensive aim with an aggressive, offensive strategy. This strategy has not been pressed exclusively by military force, but it invariably has involved emanations of military power. Historians have never questioned the role of the Red Army in the incorporation of the Eastern European buffer states into the postwar version of the Russian Empire. Southward and to the east, the Soviet Union pressed its agenda of expansion with the attempted annexation in 1945-46 of Iranian Khorasan and with the expropriation of the Sakhalin Islands from Japan as part of the peace settlement.

The persistence with which the Soviet leaders continue to press their rim-land agenda derives from motivations deep in the national psychology, motivations that are not readily susceptible to melioration by discussion at summit conferences or arms control meetings.[9] The Soviet Union's continuing pursuit of its rim-land agenda could bring it one way or another—clumsily (as in Afghanistan) or deftly (as in its cultivation of German Ostpolitik since the 1960s), by way of foreign military assistance (as in Vietnam) or by intimidating emanations of power (as in finlandization)—into conflict with U.S. interests in three regions:

1. The region of United States's special relationships, especially with the members of the so-called Atlantic Community;
2. The region of critical resource dependency, particularly the Persian Gulf; and
3. The region of emerging primacy in any plan for an expanding, open international economy: the dynamic Western Pacific region from Korea and Japan through the Association of South East Asian Nations (ASEAN) to resource-rich Australia, and certainly not excluding China.

These are regions of critical interest to the United States from the standpoints of resource dependency and overseas trade. They broadly correspond to the three strategic zones of U.S. military planning: Western Europe, Middle East, and Western Pacific. Because they also correspond to the areas of the Soviet Union's rim-land agenda, these regions contain the most likely points of action and reaction, of pressure and counterpressure between the superpowers. They coalesce into a single broad arc of intersecting—and essentially opposed—Soviet and U.S. interests.

Given that the Soviet Union must be expected to keep pressing its rim-land agenda, but given the decreasing likelihood of its doing so by means of bolt-from-the-blue aggression, in what form is the Soviet geostrategic threat to U.S. geoeconomic interests most likely to be expressed?

The Nature of the Threat

Cautious opportunism—with the emphasis on cautious—is the Soviet style. Indeed, as the successor theory to the doctrine of violent world revolution, the Soviet Union's doctrine of competitive coexistence expresses a conservative bias: a preference for exploiting chances only if they carry low costs and few risks. After all, the Soviet Union has trouble enough at home, with a faltering economy, a corrupt bureaucracy, and an apathetic citizenry, without unduly taxing its energies in foreign adventures.[10] It has ample problems with its so-called allies in Eastern Europe and with its former client, China. With limited resources to put into a campaign of world conquest, the Soviet Union looks to piecemeal moves rather than to major confrontations.

Nevertheless, major confrontations remain a possibility—not because the old bolt-from-the-blue threat is still credible, but because the Soviet war-waging doctrines open apertures to escalation in any situation of local conflict. The local piecemeal move relates to the major confrontation as a trigger relates to a gun or a fuse relates to a bomb.

Suppose that the Soviet Union sees either a local advantage to be exploited somewhere around the periphery of its territory or else a marked local threat to its own geostrategic interests. Suppose further that Soviet leaders sense a degree of U.S. irresolution, which leads them to see military force as a potentially effective means of pursuing the advantage or removing the threat. A local probe could then bring Soviet (or Soviet-proxy) forces into engagement with forces of the United States (or of U.S. allies). Engagement by proxy forces would represent a twice-displaced local war: geographically displaced from the home lands of the superpowers, and displaced from direct involvement by the real contestants because clients, rather than the principal powers, would bear the burden of actual combat.

Escalatory pressures could, at some point, bring the superpowers into direct engagement, and not necessarily in the locale of the initial probe. These escalatory pressures might take a variety of forms: the miscalculation by one side that gratuitously threatens a vital interest of the other; war hysteria or the excessive investment of national pride in the winning of a distant military contest; unpredictable political dynamics among allies—it was German-Austrian alliance dynamics that brought on World War I, and it was Axis alliance dynamics that escalated World War II; the general sense of political-military deterioration that induces the losing side to take desperate steps. Once the trigger has been pulled, once the fuse has been lit, the subsequent course of events becomes less predictable, and probably less controllable, too.

So what U.S. Pentagon planners simply call "The Threat" turns out to be a network of possible threats, threats that could involve:

1. Spread of a conventional war in one locale by way of a second Soviet (or U.S.) probe elsewhere—in effect, the ignition of a series of separate military brush fires;
2. Escalation from a local conventional war to a frontal (that is, a theaterwide) conventional war or a theater nuclear war;
3. Escalation from a theater war to a war touching the home lands of the superpowers;
4. Within the category of central war, escalation from the level of selective nuclear strikes to the level of general nuclear war (city busting, holocaust).

A different concept of threat—different from that of the bolt-from-the-blue concept—is needed to fit the more complex and subtle network of contingencies that the United States confronts in the 1980s.

A Probabilistic Imagery

Electrical engineers use the model of a switching network to describe a system in which a current in one circuit may (or may not) be switched into other circuits. Physicists use the theory of probability distribution to emphasize that a collision of elementary particles will not give a single, deterministic outcome; the trick is to predict the different probabilities of different results within a whole set of possible outcomes. Mathematicians use the Markov chain model (named after the statistician who first studied it), in which a sequence of events occurs by a series of jumps; the direction and likelihood of each jump depends on the prior state of the system. It is the same with the network of threats: A frontal move by Warsaw Pact forces against NATO Europe would be more likely to occur as an escalatory jump from a crisis over Berlin than as a bolt-from-the-blue assault on West Germany. Both the escalatory jump and the surprise assault, however, lie within the set of possible contingencies. A Soviet strike against targets in the United States would be more likely to occur as an escalatory jump from a nuclear war in Europe or the Middle East than as a bolt-from-the-blue preemptive attack. However, both the escalatory jump and the surprise attack lie—albeit with different probabilities—within the set of possible outcomes.

This concept of threat points to the need for an American political response designed to reduce the likelihood that the most probable kind of initial triggering event—the local probe—will occur. Then it points to the need for a military posture to control the subsequent course of a conflict should the political strategy fail.

A Global Political Response

The Soviet Union has a political strategy, the strategy of competitive coexistence, to guide its foreign relations: to exploit unrest in the Third World; to justify sociopathic behavior on the international stage with the claim that the Soviet Union still represents the vanguard of worldwide historical change; to secure the home land by extending Soviet influence around the borders of the Soviet Union—that is, by extending Soviet influence throughout the Eurasian rim land.

To meet this all-encompassing Soviet political strategy, the United

States needs a similarly spacious political response. A political strategy designed to promote a more peaceful world order needs to be truly global in concept—not unduly focused on the much-discussed political disarray in Europe, nor even confined to the unstable regions of the Eurasian rim land as a whole. More specifically, a global political strategy should address problems of instability—and consequent susceptibility to communist exploitation—in the Third World countries where calls for a New International Economic Order originate.[11] A global strategy also should promote change in the Soviet Union's own international role. The change that probably would do the most toward moderating and pacifying Kremlin foreign policy would involve the gradual inclusion of Soviet-bloc countries in the liberal economic order that U.S. foreign policymakers should try to revitalize. The formulation of enlightened policies to guide U.S. relations with the Third World and with potential Soviet-bloc trading partners would furnish the needed backdrop for a military posture to keep the peace around the Eurasian rim land, where the intersection of U.S. and Soviet interests raises fears of the most dangerous triggering conflicts.

Beyond the North-South Fault Line

The Soviet Union's doctrine of the changing correlation purports to explain outbreaks of social unrest beyond the North-South fault line and to appropriate the effects of such unrest to the forces that are "objectively" advancing the socialist cause. Whether the insurgents in El Salvador, Morocco, and Namibia know it or not, they are participants in the global drama of dialectical change. As protagonists in that drama, they are objectively in the communist camp.[12]

The appearance of social unrest presents an occasion for intervention by the Soviet Union or its proxies. According to the Party line, the internal contradictions of capitalism-imperialism lead to civic strife, which the repressive established authorities can only make worse by virtue of their inability to read the mandate for change; social disorder becomes politicized as leftist claimants to revolutionary leadership emerge; the self-constitution of a revolutionary shadow government enables the Soviet Union or its proxies to establish relations with an indigenous opposition group. The cultivation of influence proceeds through stages of vague political amity, provision of small arms, support with field advisers, and eventually the deployment of combat units.[13]

To the extent that the United States identifies its interests with orderly change, the aim should be to prevent this Soviet-controlled sequence from ever getting started. The aim should be to preempt the causes of the unrest that can lead first to radical politicization and then to graduated communist intervention.

Despite the contrary connotations of the word *revolution,* it takes time—years, even decades—for most Third World peoples to traverse the revolutionary path to change. Military intervention, even in the form of sale or lending of major military equipment, becomes relevant only toward the end of the process. Ironically, it is a process that often need not be permitted to reach the stage at which military intervention can prove decisive. To compound the irony, the United States should enjoy a comparative advantage in influencing the path of change at an early stage, whereas the Soviet Union arguably enjoys an advantage only after political polarization has proceeded to the point of no return and the revolution has reached a military phase. The Soviet Union's failed model of internal development offers little in the way of inspiration to the Third World revolutionaries of today, and the international communist movement that evoked such fear in the 1930s and late 1940s has spent its emotional charge. Military might, not ideological appeal or political deftness, represents the one unquestionably deployable element of the Soviet world presence.[14]

Because deteriorating situations of great interest to the United States tend to reveal themselves gradually, time should be available for efforts to divert change into constructive tracks by diplomatic-economic efforts. Only extreme cases should call for the development—on an ad hoc basis—of forces and strategies to support U.S. military intervention. The ad hoc nature of such military programs implies that they should receive ad hoc justifications in Congress and should get ad hoc funding—precisely as the U.S. military aid programs to El Salvador and Guatemala are developed and justified: as special add ons to the base-line defense effort. Taking an avowedly ad hoc approach to the advancement of U.S. interests in the Third World also would imply that no general requirement—at least not a high priority one—seems needed for force planning to meet most contingencies arising from instabilities beyond the North-South fault line.

Eliminating requirements for general military missions on the continent of Africa and in Latin America would free up resources to deal with contingencies where the process of competitive coexistence goes forward at the highest level of intensity and with the profoundest involvement of both superpowers' interests: in the area around the Eurasian rim land. Before considering the kind of military posture that the United States needs to meet contingencies around the rim land, however, it is necessary to stress the need for a political strategy aimed ultimately at converting the opposition of U.S. and Soviet interests in Eurasia into a web of compatible interests. East-West ideological competition will continue; Soviet political theory says that the antagonism must continue—albeit, under the doctrine of competitive coexistence, in abated degree. So the conversion of opposing interests into inter-dependent economic concerns can go forward only slowly. It remains important, however, even in the face of short-term setbacks (such as the failure of detente), to keep an eye on the long-term goal. The inclusion of Soviet-bloc—formally COMECON—nations in the liberal economic order would represent a step toward that goal.

Trade with the Soviet Bloc

The progressive inclusion of COMECON in an open international econ-omy would be consistent with the Soviet Union's own moves in recent years to deemphasize its traditionally autarkic policies. It needs Amer-ican grain and Western machinery. And it hopes one day to have something besides sable, vodka, and Crimean caviar to sell to the world's discriminating buyers.[15]

The gradual incorporation of the COMECON nations in a spread-ing web of global economic interdependencies would affect political relationships among Western trading partners. The recent U.S.-Eu-ropean squabbling over policies to govern high technology sales in support of the Yamal natural gas pipeline would not have occurred if the United States, like the European countries, had been competing for Soviet custom instead of trying to block East-West trade for a mixture of reasons: security reasons (not wanting the Soviet Union to build up its military with superior U.S. gadgets), economic reasons (for a while, President Reagan's advisers were touting a strategy of economic warfare), and ideological reasons (not wanting communists to enjoy the unearned fruits of capitalist technological progress).[16]

A policy of COMECON inclusion in an increasingly global free-trade zone also would affect relationships between the Soviet Union and its trading partners. Suppose that the Soviet Union and its satellites do manage to push their economies into high gear; suppose that the Soviet rates of petroleum consumption do accelerate, making the Soviet Union net importers of oil instead of modest exporters. Then the Per-sian Gulf oil fields could become objects of Soviet pressure not only as a target of expansionist opportunity—which they are now—but also as a vital economic supply area. Intensifying competition in the Persian Gulf area could touch centrally on the U.S. commitment to the Eu-ropean allies and to Japan. A Soviet probe into the Gulf, threatening economic chaos in the oil-dependent countries of Europe and Northeast

Asia, represents a more credible threat to the security of the trilateral region than does a bolt-from-the-blue attack on NATO's central front.

It is worth recalling, however, that seventeenth-century political economists believed in the ability of "sweet commerce" to tame the martial passions.[17] These thinkers expected the moderating consequences of trade to be one of the primary benefits of capitalism. The modern term for the same supposed effect is *interdependence,* which brings about relationships between trading partners in which objectives can be gained more surely by cooperative behavior—negotiation, joint ventures—than by force. According to this theory, growing COMECON reliance on Middle Eastern energy resources could temper Soviet thoughts of military probes down toward the Persian Gulf, lest military adventurism disrupt and destroy the very facilities that would represent the ostensible prize of aggression.

The Soviet Union needs high technology even more than it needs imported raw resources. It can buy what it needs from the Europeans and the Japanese, if not from U.S. businesses. Again, the process by which the Soviet Union would develop its own economic outreach, thereby becoming dependent on Italian automotive know-how, French compressor technology, German high-alloy steel, and Japanese electronics, would have a strategic by-product. Within limits, the widening of the Soviet Union's trading zone would tend to immunize its trading partners against Soviet moves that could jeopardize the flow of desired products.

Of course, after World War II the Soviet Union demonstrated a certain ability to extract technical know-how from captive German scientists. However, more recently, Poland has demonstrated that an occupied people cannot always be made to produce a net economic return. Over time, the Soviet Union might yet learn from its satellite peoples the lesson that the British taught a hundred years ago: a highly successful economic outreach often may be attained more cheaply under a regime of international trade than under a program of imperial conquest.[18] All would be gainers if U.S. policy would push the Soviet Union in that direction.

The time seems opportune for such a push. The Soviet Union is at last facing up to some of its internal problems, such as bureaucratic corruption and gross economic malperformance. How powerfully the Party leaders may feel driven to reach for radical solutions to these problems cannot be foreseen easily. Close observers of the post-Brezhnev Soviet Union, however, sense the imminence of a deep crisis and a moment of profound choice—choice between the traditional Soviet course of near-paranoid inwardness, combined with an attempted closure of the system to all that is Western, and a moderating course of interchange and interdependence with the world beyond.[19] The time seems opportune, in other words, for U.S. policymakers to take the politically courageous step that the trilateral allies have long been urging—an extension of liberal trade principles to COMECON countries in an effort to revitalize the global economic system that broke in two with the onset of bipolarity.

However, until sweet commerce with the West should gradually moderate the Soviet Union's hostility toward its erstwhile trading partners, until interdependence should gradually bring about some critical density of Soviet and American interests into alignment, the continuing opposition of interests will create the conditions for potential triggering conflicts at innummerable points around the rim land. It is mainly for action in the zone of intersecting interests around the rim land—not for pacification operations beyond the North-South fault line, or for strategic slugfests with Soviet rocket commanders—that U.S. military forces need to be designed.

Compound Instability Around the Rim Land

The argument for a carefully thought-out rim-land strategy—a strategy with both political and military components—turns on the susceptibility of rim-land areas to a dangerous condition that may be called compound instability.

Like much of the Third World, many rim-land areas have become cockpits of social unrest and political instability. The rise of Eurocommunist movements and radical "green" political parties, the depth of the cleavages that separate established power groupings from pacifist coalitions and alienated youth movements, the ambivalence of the Greek and West German commitments to the Atlantic Community, and, of course, the possibly contagious turmoil in Poland—all suggest that political instability around the rim land is not necessarily confined to the Islamic crescent of crisis and to the troubled regions of Asia. Like much of the Third World, many rim-land areas could move from civil division to political polarization to military conflict.

However, in most areas of Africa and Latin America, the Soviet Union is not well positioned to sustain long-term or high-level military involvements. Nor has it vital interests that would justify major confrontations with the United States. In Africa and Latin America, the Soviet Union prefers to make mischief and contrive embarrassments for the United States—and to do both, if possible, through proxies rather than directly. Regardless of how the United States responds to indigenous revolutionary movements or Marxist mischief making, geostrategic limits put a cap on the level of force with which the Soviet Union is likely to pursue its goals beyond the North-South fault line. By contrast, around the rim land, its geostrategic stakes and the favorable geostrategic positions of its frontal plus naval forces are such as to make escalation a real possibility. Around the rim land, the political instability that can lead to a limited local military confrontation may be compounded by the military instability that can lead to the escalatory jump.

To sum up: The United States needs a political response that addresses the problems of world order in three different areas.

Beyond the North-South fault line—that is, in Third World areas other than those that lie around the rim land—the United States should focus on the causes of political unrest by means of nonmilitary programs that promote stable economic growth. Promoting stable growth has proved a formidably difficult task in itself, and the record since World War II should not encourage anyone to think that the task is typically advanced by those who would further complicate issues by subjecting aid recipients to ideological litmus tests and then helping those who pass with large-scale military assistance. With respect to the Soviet-bloc countries themselves, continuing efforts should be made to revitalize the liberal vision through the gradual reincorporation of COMECON countries into an expanding international trading system. In the third area—around the entire Eurasian rim land—political and economic efforts also should be made toward the promotion of stable, interdependent economic growth. In this area, however, there also arises a clear-cut general (as opposed to case-by-case or ad hoc) military requirement. It is this requirement, not strategic force matching or a replay of the fascination of the 1960s with COIN warfare beyond the North-South fault line, that should drive U.S. military planning in the 1980s.

A Rim-Land Military Posture

The justification for a rim-land military emphasis within a global political strategy perhaps can best be expressed in terms of the probabilistic model of the threat. It is only around the rim land that the probabilities of severe political turmoil are compounded by the further probabilities of military engagements that also are so tightly linked to the escalatory pathways that they could lead to major superpower confrontations. (A mathematican would say that the joint probabilities of escalation through successive levels of political and military instability are high around the rim land but are low elsewhere beyond the North-South fault line—

just as, for that matter, the independent probabilities of bolt-from-the-blue Warsaw Pact or Soviet strategic rocket attacks are low.) This cascading or compounding of dangers is characteristic of the entire rim land, and it calls for a twofold definition of the U.S. military objective in any conflict. Should a Soviet or Soviet-inspired local probe upset the peace anywhere around the rim land, the United States would want both to contain the initial enemy move and to deter the larger frontal moves toward which the triggering event might otherwise lead. Similarly, should Soviet or Soviet-proxy frontal forces engage the United States's or its allies' forces, the United States would want both to contain the enemy and to deter the central strike that the Soviet Union might consider if it saw its theater strategy beginning to fail and the legitimacy of its regime called into question within the U.S.S.R.

In other words, at each of the two initial levels of possible conflict—the local level and the frontal—the United States would want to have forces capable of winning. Just as important, it would want a strategy capable of stabilizing the military situation by reducing the danger of escalation to the next higher tier of violence. Indeed, the probabilistic model suggests stability as a criterion of U.S. strategy, a criterion on par with the criteria of credibility and affordability.

The Role of Nuclear Weapons

What role should be envisioned for nuclear weapons in meeting the three-tiered threat? Will a U.S. threat of nuclear war make it less likely that the Soviet Union would, in a deteriorating local conflict, jump to a higher plane of violence? Or is there something inherently escalatory about nuclear weapons, so that the very threat of their use must evoke the imagery of exactly those consequences—perhaps even the jump to nuclear holocaust—that the threat is meant to deter?

Dulles's threat of massive retaliation evoked the imagery of holocaust in a most direct manner. However, the threat of responding to aggression with low-yield nuclear weapons—the strategy that Dulles himself eventually suggested as a way to moderate massive retaliation—also may evoke the imagery of holocaust, albeit indirectly. The celebrants of tactical nuclear weapons have never been able to allay fears that any use of these warheads inescapably threatens escalation. Tit might lead to tat, strike to counterstrike. The momentum could prove irresistable. In truth, if the irresistability of the escalatory momentum is accepted, then even the threat of an initially limited retaliatory use of nuclear warheads can have little credibility except where interests of absolutely first magnitude are at stake.

Alas, the most likely threats to U.S. interests (that is, local probes, particularly by Soviet proxies) surely lie below the threshold at which a nuclear threat is credible. If a conventional response can contain such a probe, fine. But if not? What if the level of violence should increase, say to that of a full-fledged frontal war? That possibility—to which the concept of a network of threats sensitizes one—returns the analysis to the dilemma of credibility versus affordability, because an adequate conventional response to an enemy move that escalates above the level of a local probe could be prohibitively costly.

The apparent intractability of this dilemma stems from the premise that nuclear weapons are usable—if at all—only in a retaliatory mode, only to inflict disproportionate damage on enemy targets. Indeed, such infliction inherently tends to invite escalation and thereby evokes the imagery of holocaust. From this premise, the proponents of no first use infer that the United States needs a capability for selective and proportionate responses. They infer that it needs a more controllable capability than nuclear forces ever can provide. That is, the United States needs more conventional forces, notwithstanding that its ability to meet this requirement rapidly reaches a limit set by domestic economic priorities and the allies' habitual burden shirking.

The escape from the defense dilemma, if one exists, lies in the way of a return to a strategy of nuclear resistance (instead of retaliation) as the deterrent against enemy frontal aggression. Crucial to the credibility of such a strategy would be the development of nuclear tactics for meeting oncoming Warsaw Pact units without inflicting excessive damage to noncombatants—that is, tactics and technologies for limiting a theater nuclear war.

An Imagery of Limits

The concept of limited nuclear war can never, perhaps, be fully convincing. Nor can any responsible planner suggest the use of even low-yield nuclear weapons with an altogether easy conscience. However, there are no riskless options, no easy outs. Strategy, like politics, involves ambiguous choices and compromise solutions. Despite efforts to frame a war-limiting strategy, some escalatory danger would always remain—as would the danger of enemy adventurism if the United States adopts a stance that has no credibility, and as would the dangers of so-called 'practical bankruptcy' and domestic political turmoil if it seeks to overfund its conventional posture.

As I will argue in chapter 5, a suitable compromise between credibility and affordability might require a willingness, not only to make first use of nuclear weapons in a frontal war, but also to use them much earlier in the course of hostilities than critics such as Kissinger and Solarz would want. At the same time, it would look to the development of tactics and technologies (such as enhanced radiation warheads or neutron bombs) that could permit a reasonable chance of limiting nuclear effects. In the belief that the threat of effective resistance would generate the deterrence against frontal attacks that is really sought, the main use of these battlefield nuclear weapons would be to resist enemy frontal forces rather than to inflict the disproportionate destruction that the retaliatory mode presumes.

Instead of viewing battlefield nuclear forces as a back up to conventional forces, to be used only after the latter have failed to hold an enemy frontal assault, the nuclear and the conventional forces could be seen as different kinds of tools, both to be used for resistance against invading military units rather than for retaliation, and each to be used as soon as an enemy created a tactical situation suitable for its employment. It is for this reason that the United States might use nuclear weapons without a cautionary pause, without any interim attempt to hold an enemy frontal move conventionally or to raise the threshold of nuclear initiation. (It is worth recalling that, with the strategy of vertical escalation, nuclear weapons are used only after conventional forces have lost territory. So, if this accepted strategy ever has to be used, it may succeed only in recovering real estate that has been first bloodied in unsuccessful armored infantry combat and then poisoned by nuclear fall-out.)

These strategic concepts raise doubts about the continuing relevance of some widely accepted doctrines, including the doctrines of strategic coupling; flexible response, with its implicit espousal of vertical escalation; and threshold raising, whereby the use of nuclear armament would be delayed until after a pause has permitted an attempt to hold the NATO front line conventionally. Indeed, the strategic concepts that I have advanced in the preceding paragraphs suggest nothing less than a need to reconsider those twin pillars of the U.S. military edifice, central deterrence and extended deterrence.

Central Deterrence and Extended
Deterrence Reconsidered

Today, the United States maintains a somewhat ambiguous posture of central deterrence: A triad of intercontinental ballistic missiles (ICBMs), sublaunchable ballistic missiles, and intercontinental bombers shields the U.S. home land. Simultaneously, by way of the pledge of strategic coupling, the triad helps deter a frontal attack on NATO Europe.

Instead of extending the U.S. strategic umbrella to cover the overseas theaters in this way, I submit that the United States should mount intercontinental forces for the specific and sole mission of *primary deterrence*—that is, the deterrence of any strike against the territory of the United States. Then, instead of persisting in the use of "extended deterrence," adoption of the term *secondary deterrence,* to cover both the missions of frontal deterrence and deterrence of local aggression around the Asian rim land, would emphasize that, although the security of the trilateral allies may be an important U.S. interest, it has ceased to be a central interest. Relative to its primary interest in the security of U.S. cities, the security of its trilateral allies and the security of its economic outreach represent the United States's secondary interests— interests to be protected therefore, not with U.S. strategic retaliatory forces but rather with distinct forces specially designed for nuclear resistance in Europe and for conventional resistance in Asia.

The conceptualization presented in this chapter suggests that the United States needs three special strategies, each supported by forces that are custom tailored to perform missions at a specific level of threat: a strategy of nuclear retaliation to deter an attack on the U.S. home land; a strategy of nuclear resistance against frontal aggression, with the emphasis on the European theater; and a strategy of conventional resistance to deal with local probes, mainly in the zone of the U.S. economic outreach around the Asian periphery.

In the following chapter, I present some thoughts about the kinds of forces, deployments, and tactics that could support an appropriate set of special strategies.

4 Stable Primary Deterrence

The Soviet Union reached the condition known as nuclear parity sometime in the late 1960s or early 1970s. The inevitability of the Soviet achievement had been foreseen throughout Robert McNamara's tenure as Secretary of Defense (1961-68). Even though the United States held a clear preponderance in weaponry over the Soviet Union during the 1960s, strategic planning under McNamara was dominated by the anticipation of the coming of nuclear parity, rather than by any plan to take advantage of the United States's actual—if temporary—condition of nuclear superiority.[1]

Under the anticipated conditions of superpower equivalence, a strategic attack by either side would chance not only a Western Europe overrun by the Soviet Union's frontal forces but also devastated American and Soviet home lands. The ability of either superpower to devastate the other does not require literal parity in numbers of strategic warheads. It merely requires that each side has achieved a critical threshold—the so-called threshold of assured destruction—in its long-range weaponry. Arguably, because both sides have crossed this threshold, the prospect of mutual destruction makes it irrational for the United States ever to think of hitting Soviet strategic targets unless Soviet strategic forces should have already hit targets in the United States.

A plan whereby nothing less than a strategic attack will call forth a strategic counterattack is a plan for primary deterrence stripped of the ancillary missions that U.S. strategic forces were made to carry during the era of nuclear superiority—ancillary missions such as the deterrence of local aggression by the massive retaliatory threat. In the era of nuclear parity, the sole mission of the strategic forces must be seen to be the deterrence of attacks on values so central to the survival of the United States that they justify its assumption of the ultimate risk. The erosion of the trilateral relationship bodes to complete in the 1980s what the Soviet Union, by attaining nuclear parity, started in the 1960s: a further narrowing of the mission of U.S. strategic forces by eliminating the other ancillary mission that these forces continue to bear under the doctrine of strategic coupling, the deterrence of frontal aggression against the allies.

**Mutual Assured Destruction and the
Quest for Stability**

McNamara's continuing quest for stability in the superpower balance
led to the conclusion that the United States shared with the Soviet
Union an interest in mutual invulnerability. The wrong mix of systems
in either the U.S. or the Soviet arsenal could make war more likely—
not because either superpower would want to let fly the bolt from the
blue, but because the design of one side's forces can make it either
safer for the other to strike first during a crisis or risk losing the ability
to strike at all.

During Soviet Premier Kosygin's visit to the United States in 1967,
McNamara tried to convince the Soviet leader that a stable balance
required the invulnerability of both sides' offensive forces. Each side
could then ride out an attack by the other and still have striking forces
with which to retaliate. Neither side would have a reason to launch a
preemptive attack for fear that the enemy might do so first. The achievement of invulnerability by both sides would supply the *mutual* in the
strategy called mutual assured destruction (MAD). Undeterred by the
Soviet Union's inability to see the merits of mutual destruction,
McNamara proceeded to embed MAD in U.S. strategic planning.[2]

The *assured* in the MAD formula was just as important as the
mutual. If one side could effectively resist the other's attacking force,
then it would deprive the other of the needed assured destruction
capability and hence confidence in its primary deterrent. In other words,
a special strategy of nuclear retaliation is inconsistent with a capability
for effective nuclear resistance. Inasmuch as both sides had already
begun to emphasize ICBMs as their main vehicles of strategic attack,
McNamara began to press for negotiations to forestall the further development of the antiballistic missile (ABM) systems that might permit
their possessors to neutralize the opponent's assured destruction
capability.

The Antiballistic Missile Ban

ABMs might limit the destructiveness of a central war by giving the
superpowers some defense against intercontinental weapons. As the
argument went, a full ABM program, if successfully completed by one
side, could prevent the other from credibly threatening assured destruction. The other's decision makers, foreseeing the imminent neutralization of their retaliatory capability, might launch a preemptive
strike. At minimum, they would see the need to proliferate their own

offensive forces so as to be capable of swamping the opposition's ABM, thereby further contributing to the arms race spiral.

McNamara's espousal of negotiations with the Soviet Union led to the first round of Strategic Arms Limitations Talks (SALT). To get SALT started, the principles of mutual deterrence and nuclear parity were accepted on both sides as desirable features of the military balance.[3] The Soviet Union continued to think it absurd that a nation might calculatedly expose itself to possible destruction, as McNamara's pet strategic concept of MAD required.[4] So great was the Soviet desire for an arms control treaty, however, that the Soviet Union agreed to refrain from major ABM deployments. (The terms of the ABM ban actually permitted some limited antiballistic missile emplacements, but only the Soviet Union took advantage of this proviso.)

McNamara considered the ABM ban to be a cornerstone for strategic stability. However, he also set U.S. policy on a course that was arguably inconsistent with the MAD concept that the ABM ban was supposed to support. The crucial change came in strategic targeting philosophy: in the progression from a countervalue to a counterforce and thence to a countercontrol philosphy.

Strategic Targeting

The minimum deterrence strategists of the 1950s had wanted a few good—but not necessarily very accurate—intercontinental nuclear warheads. These weapons would threaten just that supposed level of devastation, mostly in damage to Soviet cities, that would dissuade Stalin or his successors from tipping the delicate balance of terror into a state of war. Reflecting the World War II experience, the targeting theories assumed that strategic bombing meant mass terror attacks on noncombatants, that strategic bombing meant city busting.[5]

In contrast with this so-called countervalue targeting philosophy, the counterforce philosophy introduced by McNamara called for bombers and missiles to hit enemy military capabilities while minimizing collateral damage—that is, blowing up as little of the enemy's industrial plant, and killing as few Soviet noncombatants, as these enormously destructive weapons would allow.[6] Then, in July 1980, President Carter approved a further change in targeting philosophy, a change from counterforce to countercontrol.[7] His Presidential Directive (PD) 59 emphasized the destruction of those political and military command centers that constitute the central nervous system of the Soviet state. (PD 59 also retained the option of hitting the industrial centers that would be critical for the postwar recovery of the Soviet economy. In fact, since the approval of PD 59, the United States's strategic target list has grown rather than contracted, as war planners have added countercontrol and recovery denial targets to the existing counterforce target list, instead of substituting them for it.[8] In other words, under PD 59, U.S. strategic forces could be used in simultaneous strikes to disarm the enemy by counterforce targeting, to decapitate him by countercontrol targeting, and to debilitate him permanently by recovery denial countervalue targeting.)

Counterforce—and, potentially, countercontrol—suggested that, after a Soviet first strike, the United States would try to retaliate selectively. It would destroy the enemy's ability to launch yet another attack, but would not reduce his cities to piles of radioactive rubble. The Soviet Union had a fixed number of major industrial and urban centers, all vulnerable to countervalue attacks. However, the Soviet Union might proliferate its strategic rocket launchers almost limitlessly. If every new enemy missile silo had to be targeted by, say, two attacking warheads in order to ensure a kill, then both sides' adoption of counterforce meant that any increment to either's inventory of launchers would breed warhead augmentations on the other. In other words, counterforce targeting also implied strategic arms racing.

The Effect of the Multiple Independently Targetable Reentry Vehicle

In due course, the technologists devised the perfect mechanism for warhead proliferation: the multiple independently targetable reentry vehicle (MIRV). The MIRV emerged before McNamara came on the scene. It started as a U.S. device to swamp Soviet ABM systems. A limited number of launch vehicles could "spray" enemy territory with a large number of reentry vehicles, most of them unarmed decoys. Soviet defenses would simply be unable to cope. The MIRV, however, once developed, invited planners to make full use of the surprising accuracies that each of the multiple warheads—three per Minuteman III missile—could attain. Never mind that the ABM ban undercut the initial rationale of MIRV. Instead of loading U.S. warheads with duds to swamp a virtually nonexistent enemy ABM system, the military could arm them with nuclear bombs to hit the enemy's offensive rocket forces.

Without MIRV, a strike against enemy ICBMs would require the attacker to fire twice the number of missiles that were to be hit, so as to have incoming warheads in high enough numbers to allow for aiming errors and operational failures. If the first warhead should miss the enemy ICBM silo it was intended to hit, the second attacking vehicle would do the job. Owing to the need to double-target the other side's ICBMs, neither side posed a credible first strike threat against the other unless it had twice the number of missiles in the enemy's force. Mere parity in launcher numbers, therefore, contributed to stability.[9]

With MIRV, by contrast, an attacker theoretically could take out a force of x enemy ICBMs using many fewer than x missiles, with the fraction depending on the number of warheads that each attacking missile carried. Thus, one side did not even have to attain parity with the other's launcher numbers in order to pose a preemptive threat. As a result, the superpowers' failure to ban multiple warheads at the same time that they banned ABMs led to the deployment of the single most destabilizing element in the central military balance: Not the intercontinental missile itself. Not even the terrible nuclear armament that it carries. Rather, the multiple targeting capability that obscures the line between the ICBM as a preemptive threat and the ICBM as a purely retaliatory weapon.

The Vulnerability Problem

The Soviet Union eventually developed highly accurate MIRVs of their own. Their MIRV rocket forces have produced some of the same anxieties for the United States that U.S. technological prodigies continue to provoke in the Kremlin. The U.S. popularizers of these reawakened anxieties warn that 2,000 or so well-placed Soviet warheads could take out the 1,054 U.S. ICBMs in a single preemptive blow—the so-called window of vulnerability thesis.[10] Collateral strikes by Soviet sub-launched ballistic missiles (SLBMs) would also kill U.S. missile subs that are in port for refitting or crew changes and all U.S. bombers that are not on alert. Such an attack allegedly would leave such an adverse balance in the remaining U.S. strategic capabilities that the United States would have to accept face-saving truce terms. It would be finished as a world power. A clearly preponderant Soviet Union could then work its imperial will from one end of the Eurasian land mass to the other.

To some, this scenario seems implausible. Other U.S. citizens—including President Reagan—find the script credible, however. Therefore, in an excess of caution, in the early 1980s U.S. planners deemed it appropriate to consider U.S. ICBMs as—to use the buzz word—nominally vulnerable.

That nominal vulnerability of the dominant ICBM leg of the U.S. triad was really just the proxy for an interlocking set of problems. The alleged vulnerability results from the accuracy of Soviet MIRV rockets, but it is the existence of MIRVs in both sides' forces that creates the condition of instability in which either side could consider responding to a crisis by using the infernal technology to launch a first strike. Thus, MIRVs have altered the calculus of probabilities in the network of threats by increasing the likelihood of escalation from a frontal war to a central exchange. Of course, the Soviet Union would have to think much harder before striking at U.S. missiles if the United States could somehow restore its ICBMs to the invulnerability that they enjoyed before the advances in the Soviet rocket forces put them at risk. Presidents Carter and Reagan duly set forth in search of that somehow, hoping to find a restabilizing solution to the vulnerability problem that also would leave the United States with an affordable, credible primary deterrent.

Exotic Basing Plans

Under President Carter's exotic basing plan, 200 new MXs (missiles experimental, with ten nuclear warheads apiece) would have been shuttled among 4,600 launch sites in the Great Basin region of Nevada and Utah, setting up a titanic shell game to prevent the Soviet Union from knowing which launchers they should target in a preemptive strike. Alas, the citizens of Nevada and Utah preferred not to have their states scarified by the excavations of the construction workers who would build the shell-game apparatus, let alone by the Soviet warheads that might eventually be fired to wreck it. In 1981, the enormous economic and political costs of shell gaming led Congress to put the MX missile on hold, at least until a new basing mode could be found.

MXs with shell gaming would have closed the so-called window of vulnerability, but at stupendous cost (upwards of $60 billion), and by proliferating U.S. warheads in a way that the Soviet Union's commitment to parity would probably have led them to match. Instead of shell gaming the new missiles, MXs could be retrofitted to existing Minuteman silos in Montana and the Dakotas or else be clustered in the so-called dense pack configuration.

Members of a presidential commission chaired by Lieutenant General Brent Scowcroft, who had previously served as national security adviser to Gerald Ford, recommended putting one hundred MXs in superhardened silos. Notwithstanding the reassuring ring to that prefix *super,* however, it is generally conceded that existing silos cannot be hardened sufficiently to withstand Soviet warhead blasts. In mid-1983, Congress gave tentative approval to the Scowcroft plan, which would increase the U.S. warhead inventory (one hundred new MX launchers, one thousand new warheads), but would not increase those warheads' survivability. Politically, a go-ahead for MX in some form at least would have the merit of showing resolve, that is, displaying a willingness to answer a long-term Soviet rocket build up with a U.S. upgrading effort. But strategically, the MX plan seems more likely to increase instability than to achieve the opposite.

Under the alternative dense pack siting plan, one hundred MXs would have been hidden in plain sight amidst a thousand or so dummy ICBMs within a six-square-mile launch area in Wyoming. Dense pack, however, assumed too many unverified effects during a nuclear attack, such as that incoming Soviet warheads would destroy one another when they exploded, leaving the U.S. retaliatory force intact. So, under the shell gaming, the retrofitting, and the dense pack basing schemes for MX, the United States either would punish itself economically and fuel the arms race or else—to the extent that the window of vulnerability hypothesis has merit—remain imperiled by an unanswered Soviet strategic rocket threat.

Launch on Warning

There remains, of course, a way other than exotic basing to ensure the invulnerability of U.S. land-based missiles, should the United States want to continue relying on ICBMs as the main leg of its triad. Posturing a large force of U.S. missiles for launch on warning could help a little.[11] The Soviet Union then could not take out U.S. missiles because they would be launched as soon as U.S. radar screens picked up the blips that might be caused by incoming warheads (they also might be caused by migrating Canadian geese). Launch on warning, however, could hurt a lot by reducing stability. With the United States's adoption of a hair-trigger reaction policy, the balance of terror would become perhaps unsustainably delicate.

Launch on warning would show the Soviet Union the folly of its having mounted a threat to the land-based leg of the U.S. triad and, thus, would carry some of the same political merit that the MX plan does. However, launch on warning would convey this useful lesson to the Kremlin planners by adding to the uncertainties of the central military balance. It is a balance under which the United States as well as the Soviet Union must live. It is as much in the United States's interest to preserve the steadiness of that balance as it would be to achieve a (probably temporary) tilt in its favor. Again, a sober assessment of the stakes suggests that no solution to the alleged vulnerability problem should be bought at the cost of violating the criterion of stability.

Single-Warhead Mobile Missiles

In early 1983, Henry Kissinger proposed an alternative plan for upgrading the ICBM leg of U.S. strategic triad, a form of above-ground shell gaming that the Scowcroft commissioners also accepted as an add on to their MX retrofitting scheme.[12] Kissinger's version of shell gaming, however, attempts to ensure the invulnerability of U.S. ICBMs while explicitly dealing with the problem of instability in the central balance. The key to Kissinger's plan for strategic stabilization lies in the fact that parity in non-MIRV missile forces spells stability, whereas parity with MIRVs leads to the opposite. Kissinger would scrap the MX out of hand and arm a new generation of small intercontinental missiles (Midgetmen) with a single warhead apiece. By focusing on the gradual elimination of MIRVs, the United States would set the stage for arms control negotiations aimed at mutual cutbacks to lower and lower numbers of ICBMs. Such a scheme would dovetail nicely with the downbuilding process that has been espoused by leading U.S. senators, such as Cohen of Maine and Nunn of Georgia. A downbuilding agreement with the Soviet Union would require that every new warhead added to either side's strategic inventory be accompanied by the retirement of two existing warheads.[13]

The invulnerability of Kissinger's non-MIRV ICBMs would be preserved by moving both armed and decoy Midgetmen around on trucks, so as to confuse the enemy. For every armed missile, up to a dozen fakes also would be shuttled about. Even if the Soviet Union were able to monitor the comings and goings of U.S. launchers, it could not tell which missiles to target. By the tests of survivability and of stability, the Kissinger plan would represent an improvement over MX deployment in existing silos. Like MX, however, it would commit the United States to a whole new generation of land-based missiles and hence to the perpetuation of a full triad of strategic systems at precisely the moment in history when U.S. ICBMs arguably should be deemphasized in favor of cheaper, simpler, more survivable alternative systems.

Why, after all, do the Kissingers and Scowcrofts insist that the United States move forward to a new generation of ICBMs, whether in the form of MXs with MIRVs or in the form of single-warhead Midgetmen? At bottom, support for ICBM upgrading depends on a particular theory of the strategic posture that the United States would need to retaliate after a Soviet first strike. It is that theory, as well as the ICBM force that would support it, that needs reassessment.

To Support the Retaliatory Mission

Under the MAD concept, a Soviet attack would call for a suitable level of assured destruction to be inflicted on the Soviet Union (the retaliatory component of the counterstrike). At the same time, the United States would want to inhibit the Soviet Union's ability to deliver yet additional blows by hitting at the remaining Soviet strategic forces (in effect, a resistive component, which also is a war-waging component). Those who emphasize the war-waging component of the U.S. strategic posture see a need for many accurate, invulnerable ICBMs that can ride out an enemy first strike and then hit time-urgent Soviet targets— specifically, unlaunched enemy rockets. It is a persuasive interpretation of the strategic mission if invulnerability on this order (that is, sufficient to permit the full riding out of an attack) can be afforded, and if the United States really wants the Soviet Union to think that its rocket forces as well as the U.S. ICBMs are radically at risk.

The case can be made, however, for an alternative strategy. An alternative strategy would seek for a lesser order of invulnerability in U.S. strategic forces, but an affordable one; it would adjust the balance between retaliatory and war-waging counterattack plans by targeting mainly Soviet control and some recovery denial objectives in the second strike—that is, by signaling a limited war-waging intention—while simultaneously finding ways to signal the United States's desire not to escalate to the holocaust of countervalue exchanges. It would contribute to stability by displaying the United States's desire not to put the Soviet rocket capability radically at risk, and it would permit the United States to begin downsizing its ICBM force.

Downsizing the ICBM Force

Redesigning the ICBM force primarily for selective raid-type strikes, instead of as a major counterforce threat to the huge Soviet strategic rocket force, could permit the existing U.S. missile fleet to be downsized. In order to promote stability, the U.S. warhead inventory should be small enough to pose no credible first strike threat against the Soviet land-based missile force. However, it should be large enough so that it poses an assured second strike threat to a limited menu of counter-control, recovery denial, and maybe some selective counterforce targets. The Midgetman development would represent a step in the right direction, and surely one preferable to MX development—but, nevertheless, it would be an unnecessary step, because the limited war-waging mission could be handled by existing Minutemen. Indeed, the limited war-waging mission could be handled by a much smaller force of Minutemen than the one thousand missiles now kept on line, provided that such a smaller force were upgraded with state-of-the-art guidance systems to qualify them for selective sharpshooter raids.

Reducing the level of the preemptive threat that each side poses against the other is the key to stabilizing the central balance. The preemptive capability of a missile force can be assessed on the basis of its targeting accuracies and on the basis of its number of offensive warheads relative to the number of counterforce targets (that is, enemy rocket launchers). U.S. ICBMs do need high accuracies if they are to be able to make selective strategic strikes, whether of the counterforce or countercontrol variety. The high accuracies that a limited war-waging force would require leaves the number of warheads on U.S. ICBMs as the variable in the missile force that must be adjusted as a way of easing Soviet fears of a first strike. The course toward stability lies in cutting back on the number of highly accurate, potential first strike warheads that pose the real menace to the strategic rocket forces on which the Soviet Union relies for primary deterrence against a U.S. attack. The course toward stability lies in a cutback to beneath the threshold of warhead numbers at which U.S. ICBMs can pose a credible first strike threat to the Soviet land-based force. The course toward stability with affordability lies in reliance on upgraded versions of the existing Minutemen rather than in building to the first strike threshold with an all-new system such as the Midgetman.

The United States needs a few good intercontinental missiles, with the measure of the term *few* set by the first strike threshold. That first strike threshold would be the target of the gradual downsizing program. The resultant trimming of the U.S. ICBM force could proceed by unilateral action, but it would suggest further negotiated bilateral ICBM cutbacks, with the understanding that Soviet reductions would elicit additional U.S. reductions, in decrements that would tend to keep a stable no-first-strike ratio between the two forces.

In order to promote stability in the central balance, then, U.S. force planning should move away from the objective of a strategic triad in the mirror-image of the Soviet Union's, one that matches the Soviet intercontinental rocket capability almost on a launcher-for-launcher, or even a warhead-for-warhead, basis. Should it, furthermore, move beyond the very conception of a triad of ICBMs, sublaunchable missiles, and bombers? Indeed, there are those who would put U.S. force planning on a considerably more radical course than that of mere downsizing of the ICBM structure. Some of the country's best defense thinkers—

M.I.T. scholar William Kaufmann, for example, and General Maxwell Taylor—would move to transfer the assured destruction capability to the already invulnerable missile-firing submarines.[14]

Upgrading the Submissile Force

Under a procurement schedule that is already underway, the 1980s will see the U.S. fleet of aging Polaris and Poseidon submarines upgraded through the rapid addition of the most advanced Trident-class boats. The new submarines, when equipped with the Trident II SLBMs, could virtually substitute for a land-based MX force, in the sense that the improved warhead accuracies of the Trident IIs would permit them to pick up the counterforce mission of accurately hitting hardened, time-urgent Soviet military targets.

However—even aside from the possibility that the U.S. submarine force could be made vulnerable by some (now unforeseen) break-through in Soviet anti-submarine warfare (ASW) capabilities—there remain reasons why neither a large-scale nor a limited strategic war-waging mission should be loaded onto U.S. submarines. These reasons have to do with the special suitability of the submarine fleet to carry the weight of the ultimate deterrent.

The ultimate deterrent lies not in the Kremlin leaders' foreknowl-edge that Soviet preemption would bring retaliation against a specific set of economic, military, or political targets. Strike and counterstrike calculations no doubt figure in the reckonings of top political leaders. However, the ultimate deterrent lies in the generalized, visceral fear of a holocaust in which millions of Soviet and U.S. citizens would die as a consequence of each side's last ditch acts of retaliation against cities. In the same way that battlefield nuclear and conventional weapons should, in general, be reserved for those missions that they can re-spectively best perform, U.S. missile-launching submarines and ICBMs should be ticketed specifically for those strategic missions that they can best perform—last ditch countervalue retaliation by the submarines, and limited war-waging strikes by highly accurate sharpshooter ICBMs.

Such a division of mission would have its grounding in a particular theory of warfare, a theory that highlights the enormous unpredicta-bility of all combat situations. This pervasive element of unpredictability means that the United States must prepare to meet a variety of possible contingencies. If it prepares multipurpose weapons systems to meet various contingencies, then the use of a given weapons system will not clearly signal an understanding of the nature of the contingency that is being met. If the United States intends to make a limited strike, in the hope that such a strike would accurately signal a finely shaded mixture of resolve and restraint, then it should not have to do so by using a weapons system that the enemy might mistake for the instrument of a wholesale city-busting attack.

Let us consider this theory of warfare, and its implications for U.S. strategic force planning—specifically, its implications for the proposal to upgrade the U.S. submarine-missile fleet.

A Theory of Central War

Notwithstanding the best efforts of the war gamers, it cannot be predicted beforehand just how many strikes, or what kinds of exchanges, might intervene between the outbreak of a central war and the final paroxysm of a countercity exchange. No one really knows if the chemistry of nuclear generalship would drive decision makers toward all-out exchanges, toward a kind of nuclear-style attempt to fight classical counterforce battles, or even toward the use of strategic weapons in limited numbers to take out isolated targets. A British general, Sir John Hackett, has convincingly developed the scenario of a global war in which just two nuclear countervalue strikes—by the Soviet Union against Birmingham, England, followed by a NATO retaliatory attack on Minsk—prove so demoralizing that all fronts just collapse.[15]

The adversaries may not try to destroy each other as organized societies. They may not even try to destroy each other's war-waging capabilities. Selective, possibly sporadic nuclear strikes might be used to punctuate a sustained political crisis without escalating to a holocaust. Singular strikes might be reciprocated in a Hackett-type war that the contestants tacitly agree to keep mostly conventional. Decision makers who trust in the accuracy of their weaponry might risk selective raid-type attacks while hoping to contain the escalatory pressures that could lead to major nuclear counterforce strikes. (Suppose that, in a ghastly reprise of the outbreak of World War I, "the lamps begin to go out" and the Soviet Union knocks out Sault Ste. Marie—an important but remote pressure point in the North American economy. If U.S. radar screens show just one missile, not a hail of warheads, coming in, does SAC hit back with everything it has? Or does it respond in kind—say, by putting just one missile on the new Soviet hydro plant in Bratsk?) The objective in a nuclear raid would be not to disarm the opponent but rather to affect the resolution of a crisis by selectively neutralizing specific enemy capabilities seriatim or by influencing the enemy's perception and will.

The script for a future war cannot be predicted with any confidence. One cannot know if going nuclear in a frontal war would end up involving the superpowers in a central exchange; one cannot know if a central nuclear exchange could remain limited. This unpredictability implies the need to build flexibility into the U.S. strategic retaliatory force by considering a range of options. The ICBM component is ideally suited to give the United States a capability to exploit one particular option. The submarine component can be tailored for another one, albeit one complementary to that reserved for U.S. land-based missiles.

The Complementary Missions

It is for the limited war-waging mission—selective, accurate, time-urgent strikes—that the ICBM is best suited. Of course, both contestants would face a potentially catastrophic epidemiological problem if the frequency or number of firings by either side gave rise to a sense of exponential increase in the scale of conflict, leading to the ultimate countervalue exchange. Both contestants would, therefore, have incentives to keep the war from accelerating as a function of its own gathering speed, as occurs in epidemics. The final city-busting exchange might be the third, fourth, or nth strike rather than the second. The longer the delay between the first strike and the nth strike, the better might be the chance that the ultimate countervalue exchange will not occur at all, particularly if the persisting threat of a final city-busting exchange can help to restabilize an ongoing conflict by stopping it short of mutual annihilation.

However bad limited missile strikes against enemy military forces might seem, decision makers should know that their countries will suffer far worse if the war escalates to last ditch countervalue exchanges. The best way to convey this knowledge to the Soviet Union would be to preserve the strategic submarine force as an exclusive instrument of the ultimate threat. In other words, the mission of the strategic submarine force should be to confirm the incentives for restraint by threatening an assured capability for last ditch retaliation even in the context of an ongoing war.

U.S. strategists have, in the main, rejected this concept, known as intrawar deterrence.[16] They fear that the first nuclear step would almost inevitably carry both combatants all the way up the ladder of escalation. Theories of intrawar deterrence, and kindred theories of limited nuclear war waging, do little more than tincture strategic thought. Even as a tincture, however, the theory that a central nuclear war could be contained by the intrawar deterrent of an invulnerable, unused last ditch retaliatory threat, deserves notice. It calls attention to the need for a system of buffers against escalation from selective strikes to general holocaust in the event that primary deterrence should fail.

To put the matter more precisely, *stable primary deterrence* itself has multiple levels of meaning. It means, in the first instance, that the United States should deter any attack on its home land. It also means that the United States should never have an incentive to consider striking first against the Soviet Union, thereby inviting retaliation. Furthermore, it means that, failing the prevention of an initial strike by either side, the United States should give the enemy an incentive to limit his blows. This can be best accomplished—again, there are no guarantees—both by limiting U.S. strikes against the Soviet homeland and by withholding the last ditch retaliation against cities that would leave the Soviet Union nothing to lose by letting fly back with everything that it has left.

A Submarine Final Force

To maintain a credible threat of last ditch retaliation, the final deterrent force must be known to be capable of surviving all attempts to destroy it. It must remain (as the operational types express it) connected, so that some residuum of the nation's political leadership can give the order for final retaliation, should that extreme measure be deemed appropriate. Optimally, it would remain on station in an area such as the Indian Ocean, from which missile trajectories could be clearly distinguished from the transpolar trajectories of the counterforce weapons (ICBMs and bombers) that are based in the continental United States.

However, given certain operational characteristics that a final force would not need in order to hit Soviet cities—it would not need a large warhead inventory; it would not need high targeting accuracies—the force that is ticketed for last ditch retaliation probably should be the missile-firing submarine force that more or less already exists, that is, the existing Polaris and Trident I missiles should not be replaced by the more accurate Trident IIs. The Polarises and Trident Is now in the fleet do not have pinpoint capabilities, but city busting needs no such accuracies. On the other hand, equipping U.S. strategic submarines with Trident IIs would meet the technical requirements of a force intended for time-urgent missions requiring high targeting accuracy—precisely the capabilities that the United States does not want in its final force, because U.S. submarines would then present a destabilizing first strike counterforce threat to the Soviet land-based missiles. The submarines' capability to do so would compromise their ability to serve as an identifiable final force for use only in extremis.

The U.S. missile-firing submarine force has been merchandized as a nearly invulnerable all-purpose deterrent. It would be unrealistic to look for a cutback in the force to the minimal level that would be necessary for the ultimate retaliatory mission—which could, in fact, prove to be a low level indeed: A single Trident submarine carries enough warheads to level every major Soviet population and industrial center. Even if the existing strategic submarine force is not subjected immediately to heroic retirements, it—like the U.S. ICBM force—should be decreased gradually. U.S. planning should be guided by a disposition to signal that U.S. missile submarines will be increasingly dedicated to the mission for which they have a comparative advantage, the last ditch mission.

Between Singular Strike and Nth Strike

Put it, then, that a small force of highly accurate ICBMs—preferably existing Minutemen retrofitted with single warheads—would be ticketed for the limited war-waging mission of undertaking raid-type singular and selective strikes. A small force of sublaunchable missiles would be reserved from use as the United States's nth strike threat—its last ditch retaliatory capability. These two specialized missions leave a range of missions in between sporadic raid-type attacks and last ditch city busting. How should this intermediate range of missions be covered? I believe that, even as ICBMs with MIRVs and counterforce-capable sublaunchable missiles are deemphasized, manned bombers should be reemphasized as the backbone of a modest-size strategic striking force.

A Strategic Striking Force

Unlike an ICBM-intensive force postured for launch on warning, a bomber-intensive force postured for launch under attack can permit an acceptable compromise between survivability and stability. Unlike an ICBM-intensive force that has been rendered invulnerable through the adoption of an exotic basing scheme, a bomber-intensive force also can represent an acceptable compromise between survivability and affordability.

A mixed ICBM-bomber force probably would not, for example,

have the survivability of MXs in a shell-game basing mode. The recommended downsized Minuteman force in existing silos would, by hypothesis, be vulnerable if the Soviet Union elected to hit U.S. ICBMs in an all-out preemptive strike (instead of targeting them seriatim in a series of selective exchanges). And the nonalert bombers in a strategic striking force probably would not get off at all. The primary reliance on aircraft, however, would enable a significant fraction of the retaliatory force—that is, alert bombers—to be launched, subject to recall, as soon as U.S. radar screens showed the possibility of a Soviet attack. No subject-to-recall promises can be attached to the launch order for ICBMs, which is why the mixed force that has bombers as its backbone more than pays for its reduced survivability with a gain in stability.

The exact degree of survivability of U.S. bombers under a Soviet first strike would depend on the speed with which incoming missiles could knock out American air bases, relative to the speed with which the bomber force could be flushed. This kill-to-flush relationship can be altered by variations in the bomber alert status and, of course, in the attack plan that the Soviet Union might use.

To minimize the percentage of the American bomber force that could be scrambled under attack, the Soviet Union presumably would want to minimize the time between the United States's receipt of tactical warning (those radar blips again) and the Soviet missiles' detonations on target. Therefore, SAC's air bases generally are assumed to be targeted by Soviet missile-firing submarines cruising close to U.S. waters. These submarines' SLBMs may not be particularly accurate weapons. But, then air bases make large, soft aiming points. Taking likely SLBM trajectories into account, it commonly is estimated that ten minutes of warning would be available for flushing U.S. bombers upon notice of a Soviet attack.[17] (If the Soviet Union were to fire strategic rockets from its home land, so as to strike U.S. missile silos at the same moment that its SLBMs hit U.S. air bases, the thirty-minute transpolar trajectories would extend the United States's tactical warning, enabling more of the U.S. bomber fleet to scramble.)

The different estimated mean flight times of attacking SLBMs and land-based rockets (ten minutes versus thirty minutes), and their appropriate counterforce targets (U.S. air bases versus U.S. missile silos), opens a kind of window of vulnerability for the Soviet Union. It would take nerve, and would imply considerable risk, for the United States to exploit that window. However, it would take less nerve and imply a lower level of risk for the United States to do so than it would for the Soviet Union to launch the preemptive strike that would start the script running.

The Launch under Attack Strategy

It generally is considered that the Soviet Union's best chance for a successful disarming strike would involve the simultaneous launching of its SLBMs and strategic rockets. Simultaneous launching would minimize the survivability of the U.S. bomber force. However, simultaneous Soviet launches would still leave ten minutes of warning to flush the highest possible percentage of U.S. aircraft. Another ten to fifteen minutes would be available for assessing the damage caused by the first wave of Soviet SLBMs before Soviet rockets on the transpolar trajectory hit U.S. cities or military forces. This ten-to-fifteen-minute period should permit the United States to make a rough estimate of damage to the U.S. air-base system, suggesting the extent—and something, therefore, of the intent—of the Soviet attack. Any U.S. ICBM firings probably would have to be ordered during this period, because U.S. silos would be vulnerable to the incoming Soviet warheads, unless the nation opted for an inordinately expensive basing mode, such as shell gaming.

The scale of the U.S. counterattack in response to a major Soviet counterforce strike would depend on the mix of bombers and ICBMs in the U.S. strategic striking force, on the degree of bomber alertness, and on the disarming effect of the Soviet SLBM strike. If the attack left more rather than fewer U.S. bases intact, more rather than fewer flushed aircraft could be recalled. Thus, launch under attack would have a certain automaticity (read: credibility). The preemptive destruction of U.S. bases virtually would force some of the aircraft on to their targets, and in numbers bearing a proportion to the extent of the destruction done by the Soviet first strike.

A bomber-intensive strategic striking force postured for launch under attack would split the difference, as it were, between the high level of stability implied by an invulnerable but very costly striking force (that is, MXs with shell gaming) and the extreme delicacy implied by a cheaper but vulnerable ICBM force with launch on warning. The mixed striking force represents the best compromise for a primary deterrent that satisfactorily meets the criteria of stability, credibility, and affordability. In the main, it could be brought into existence using existing systems—no MXs nor Midgetmen, but rather upgraded single-warhead Minutemen in existing silos; no Trident II missiles, but rather SLBMs that are already in the fleet. Advanced bombers (probably the Stealth aircraft, which already is far along in development) would represent the only new starters. Even then, Stealth need be procured only in numbers needed to give the country a large enough alert bomber force to carry the intermediate range of missions—that is, countercontrol, counterforce, and some recovery denial countervalue strikes—between highly selective raids and last ditch retaliation.

An Asymmetrical Superpower Match Up

The United States's movement in the direction of a mixed striking force would result in a vastly more asymmetrical superpower match up than exists today—a bomber-intensive American force confronting a Soviet triad in which land-based missiles predominate. Neither the U.S. nor the Soviet force, however, would be noticeably inferior in deterrent or war-fighting capabilities. And—of controlling importance—each force would enjoy much greater survivability than would the symmetrical MIRV-intensive forces toward which the United States and the Soviet Union have been heading. Thus, the asymmetrical balance also would be the more stable one.

From Triad to Dyad

To get from the symmetrical to the asymmetrical cases, it will be necessary for the United States to cross walk from the strategic triad as traditionally conceptualized by U.S. planners to a dyad of forces: a strategic striking force consisting of ICBMs and bombers, a small final force of missile-firing submarines, and a buffer in between—a buffer marked out primarily by the invulnerability, the smallness, and the differentiability of the U.S. final force (see table 4–1).

The United States's movement toward a strategic dyad of this description would work to stabilize the central balance, even in the absence of further arms agreements between the superpowers. None of which is to suggest that any effort can be spared in negotiating with the Soviet Union for continuing mutual strategic arms reductions. However, the SALT I treaty was difficult to negotiate. It was exceedingly limited in its accomplishments. And—as MIRVs demonstrated—it missed altogether what really should have been both sides' negotiating target, a ban on destabilizing multiple warheads. SALT II proved even more difficult to write and then failed to be ratified in the U.S. Senate.[18] So, until the next round of negotiations produces concrete results, the course of responsible statecraft lies in the taking of unilateral steps toward a credible and affordable primary deterrent that promotes stability in the central military balance.

Nor does the design for a strategic dyad—a striking force and a final force—necessarily commit the United States (or humankind in

Table 4–1
Critical Components of U.S. Strategic Force Structure under Alternative Strategies

	Strategic Triad		Strategic Dyad Late 1980s-Early 1990s	
	Current Level	Late 1980s-Early 1990s	Striking Force	Final Force
ICBMs				
Titan	52	–	–	
Minuteman II	450	100	–	
Minuteman III	550	550	300	
MX	–	100	–	
Midgetman	–	250	–	
Manned bombers				
FB-111	60	–	–	
B-52G	151	120	120	
B-52H	96	96	–	
B-1	–	100	–	
Stealth	–	–	100	
Total striking force	1,359	1,316	520	
Warheads on line				
In single reentry vehicles	502	350	300	
In three-warhead MIRVs	1,650	1,650	–	
In ten-warhead MIRVs	–	1,000	–	
Gravity bombs	2,160	3,920	2,000	
Tomahawk-As	–	3,000	2,400	
Warheads in striking force	4,312	9,920	4,700	
Missile submarines				
Polaris	8	–		–
Poseidon	31	31		12
Trident	3	11		11
Total final force	42	42		23
Of which dedicated to North Atlantic	31	31		–
Of which dedicated to Asian Main West of Malacca Strait	–	–		23
North of Malacca Strait	9	9		–
Warheads on line				
In pre-Trident SLBMs	1,296	912		–
In Trident Is	2,640	2,280		4,560
In Trident IIs	–	2,280		–
Warheads in final force	3,936	5,472		4,560

Source: Author's estimates adapted from *U.S. Military Posture for FY 1982* (Washington, D.C.: U.S. Government Printing Office, 1981), 44, 70-71; Caspar Weinberger, *Annual Report to Congress for FY 1983* (Washington, D.C.: U.S. Department of Defense, 1982), III-59-61.

general) to an indefinite existence under the Strangelovian rubric of mutual assured destruction. But proposals for work on space-age defenses against intercontinental rockets and missiles rely on an effort of uncertain technical feasibility, unmeasured cost, and unquestionable destabilizing potential.[19] Eventually, so-called Star Wars defenses could usher in an era of resistive strategies even at the level of a central conflict by making it possible to think of military forces going against opposing military forces with such success as to virtually eliminate the retaliatory fear. In theory, such defenses—laser shields and directed energy beams—could ensure mutual survival rather than mutual destruction, even under an all-out missile exchange. Either side's attainment of reliable antimissile defenses before the other's, however, would merely evoke the scenario of preemptive attacks that McNamara outlined in the 1960s, when he made out the case against the first generation of U.S. and Soviet ABMs.

In any event, a stable superpower balance in a post-MAD era lies beyond the horizon of existing weaponry and probably would require the creation of new multilateral political institutions to guide the development and dispersal of advanced protective technologies.[20] The prudent course for now lies in a restoration of MAD, albeit in a form that radically changes the way the United States projects its strategic concepts—the concepts of primary deterrence and nuclear retaliation—into its strategic force structure.

5 On NATO's Central Front

Since the early 1960s, when flexible response replaced massive retaliation as the United States's guiding strategic concept in the event of a conflict overseas, local deterrence—in the sense of the threat to take nuclear reprisals as punishment for low-level aggression—has been excluded from the list of appropriate applications of U.S. strategic forces. Under the doctrine of strategic coupling, however, U.S. ICBMs and long-range bombers remain committed to the secondary mission of deterring a Warsaw Pact armored assault against NATO Europe. Plainly, the strategic mission cannot be narrowed to the limited one of primary deterrence so long as the United States continues to make U.S. cities hostages on behalf of its allies' security.

The narrowing of the mission of U.S. strategic nuclear forces to that of primary deterrence would leave a vacuum at the second tier of the threat, the level of frontal aggression. The United States must fill this vacuum while gradually withdrawing the pledge of strategic coupling and while settling the divisive doctrinal controversy over first use of battlefield nuclear weapons. To do all this will require a set of specialized concepts and tactics geared to the mission of frontal deterrence along the border that divides the Warsaw Pact countries from West Germany.

The Continuing German Problem

Although the United States's promise to use nuclear weapons in defense of its allies extends to all of the Atlantic partners—most particularly, to its "best ally," Great Britain, and its "first ally," France—it is clear that West Germany's crucial geopolitical position endows the Federal Republic with a peculiar mixture of military vulnerability and strategic importance.[1] Today, as in the immediate aftermath of World War II, a stable Europe depends on a politically and strategically stable Federal Republic. Today, as then, a stable Europe is the cynosure of U.S. policy toward the so-called Atlantic Community. Frontal deterrence along the border between the Germanies continues to be a U.S. military objective, because it is a means toward achieving a broader political purpose: the stabilization of the peace of Europe.

The system that grew out of the Yalta Agreements had as its primary purpose the stabilization of the peace that Germany had upset five times between 1860 and 1940. The "protective glacis" of satellite states between the Soviet Union and West Germany became a vital component of the postwar European system.[2] Other vital components were the partial dismemberment of Germany, by which East Prussia and Silesia were absorbed into Poland; the division of what remained of Germany into eastern and western zones; and, later, the matching admissions of the Federal and Democratic Republics into the NATO and Warsaw Pact alliances.

The obliteration of Germany as a force in international relations was considered as a possible solution to the German problem, as was full German integration into a united Europe. In 1945, Stalin wanted to impose a carthaginian peace on Germany, but Churchill and Roosevelt prevented the creation of a total power vacuum in central Europe.[3] In 1955, the United States wanted a unified Franco-German army, but France insisted on distancing its military posture from that of West Germany.[4] The Germans would have preferred reunification all along, but they had to settle for the Mutual Recognition Treaty of 1972, Ostpolitik, and the 1975 Helsinki Accords. Thus, the situation has been one of adjustment and countermove, always halting short of a "solution." A continuing series of military and political adjustments has occurred, cumulatively aimed at maintaining a tolerable degree of stability.

Partial West German Rearmament

The partial rearmament of West Germany—*partial* being the key term—fit into the pattern of incremental, piecemeal adjustment.

German remilitarization, which all of the Yalta conferees assumed would be impermissible for years into the future, had become, within a decade of the end of World War II, an imperative of Western policy. After the Korean invaders staged an apparent rehearsal for possible offensives elsewhere around the periphery of the communist bloc, Western policymakers came to believe that aggression in Europe would most likely come in military rather than political form—as the bolt-from-the-blue move against the central front. Accordingly, American, British, and French planners made some calculations of the military balance in Europe. After taking Soviet (and prospectively, total Warsaw Pact) manpower superiority into account, they determined that West German divisions should be fielded in numbers sufficient to equilibrate the confronting forces.[5]

At no time, however, did the Western powers contemplate an independent nuclear capability for the Federal Republic. Nor did West Germany apparently covet one. Whether the Soviet Union or, for that matter, France would have tolerated German acquisition of the bomb, or just what they might have done if West Germany had tried for a nuclear capability of its own, remain moot issues. Surely, however, full German rearmament would have proved severely upsetting.

The tacit agreement by all parties to limit German rearmament, an essential ingredient in the formula for stabilization, had an inescapable result: It necessitated a singular U.S. commitment to a posture of extended nuclear deterrence, hinged on the doctrine of strategic coupling.

Extended Deterrence and Strategic Coupling

During the formative period of NATO planning, the minds of foreign policymakers and military thinkers were understandably fixated on the new variable in the strategic equation, the absolute weapon. Western planners accepted Bernard Brodie's argument that the terrible destructiveness of atom bombs, and the apparent impossibility of adequately defending against determined use of them, seemed to suit them particularly for employment as a retaliatory deterrent, rather than in more traditional (that is, resistive) military missions.[6]

So, by what might have seemed a perfectly logical association of ideas, the expected need to deter an assault on Europe in the aftermath of the Korean War implied the further need for a nuclear capability. In the interest of European stability, this capability had to be wielded in West Germany, where the massive frontal attack seemed most likely to come, yet not by West Germany itself. In a historical and political context that made nuclear deterrence intellectually respectable but full German rearmament unacceptable, a nuclear threat could be brought to bear on the central front only as a projection of American power thousands of miles beyond American borders, and only in the form of a posture of extended nuclear deterrence. This imperative led to the confounding of the United States's primary deterrent, the U.S. strategic retaliatory forces, with the mission of frontal deterrence. The strategy of flexible response did little to alleviate that confounding of missions. And, as I have already suggested, the doctrine of strategic coupling by which the United States pledges to continue the confounding now bodes to wreck what remains of the nation's deterrent posture in Europe on the shoal of incredibility.

The European countries—and, most particularly, the West Germans—have long recognized that their security may not remain a transcendent U.S. interest, one sufficiently weighty to draw the United States into central war. If Europeans (and some U.S. citizens) doubt the reliability of the extended pledge, why would the Soviet Union not doubt it as well? If Europe expects the U.S. resolve to soften in a crisis, why might the Soviet Union not entertain similar suspicions? Such suspicions invite probing and testing by Warsaw Pact planners. To put the point more strongly than McGeorge Bundy and his co-authors did in their celebrated Spring 1982 *Foreign Affairs* piece calling for no first use of nuclear weapons: The credibility of strategic coupling, if not already gone, is irreversibly going. The deterrent value of NATO's posture logically may go right along with it, bringing about exactly the destabilization in central Europe that all parties to the peace have tried to prevent since World War II.

The No-First-Use Alternative

According to Bundy and the other proponents of no first use, given the prospect of a Warsaw Pact attack, the NATO partners together should prepare to take their best defensive shot by strictly conventional means. If that best shot fails to hold the attackers, NATO decision makers still should refrain from initiating nuclear actions to contain the aggressors' westward sweep. This waiving of an unlimited right to raise the level of response signifies an awareness that nuclear weapons have irrecoverably altered the political calculations that should control military tactics: Henceforth, the prudent course may require, after the best shot has been taken, a willingness to lose, rather than to risk "the general nuclear war that would bring ruin to all and victory to none."[7]

Assuming that the Soviet Union also would refrain from initiation, no first use would obviate any need for the United States to put its intercontinental missiles where its nuclear pledge has been. With no first use, neither side would start the sequence that could escalate to a central exchange. More and more U.S. citizens are swinging behind Bundy's no-first-use alternative precisely because, with strategic coupling, they fear that nuclear initiation in a European ground war could trigger the escalatory sequence that ends up in a missile war between the superpowers.

Although no first use of battlefield nuclear weapons proved to be the big idea among U.S. defense thinkers in the early 1980s, the proposal has had few cheerleaders on the Continent. Most European leaders—if not most men on the street in Bonn, Paris, and London—do indeed want a battlefield nuclear strategy, preferably (from their viewpoint) in combination with a reaffirmed U.S. strategic pledge.[8] They want a battlefield first-use option for both tactical and economic reasons.

Tactically, a longstanding view in NATO is that only a battlefield nuclear threat can force Warsaw Pact planners to disperse their armored units, should they attack, so as to deny NATO defenders targets that are worthy of a nuclear response. Assertions to the effect that nuclear weapons have no military uses are sometimes heard.[9] On the contrary, the threat of a battlefield nuclear response has a profound effect on the enemy's military posture. The first-use threat forces him to mount the dispersed attacking formations that also might give NATO defenders targets capable of being handled with modest conventional forces. For this reason, preservation of the first-use option might permit the allies to win a war in Europe without going nuclear and without funding a major conventional build up.

Why is it that the United States should be concerned about the funding of such a build up? To begin with, renunciation of first use unaccompanied by a major conventional build up would trade an allegedly incredible nuclear posture for a virtual nonposture—a still-inadequate NATO conventional capability, but without either a battlefield first-use option or strategic coupling, except in the (unlikely) event that Warsaw Pact aggressors initiated nuclear use. As for the price tag on the conventional program that would be needed, recall that the U.S. Office of Management and Budget estimated that some $100 billion might have to be spent by the NATO countries in order for their combined non-nuclear forces to have a high-confidence forward defense posture on the central front.[10] Cut that estimate by a third—by half—and it still remains a frighteningly large dollar figure.

Could dollars be combined with marks and pounds to do the job? Is the call that the advocates of no first use are making for an alliancewide conventional build up realistic? If the answer is no, then how prudent would it be to declare an end to both strategic coupling and the battlefield first-use policy? Indeed, maybe the deepening sense of nuclear dread means that one of them has to go. Given the tactical, economic, and political arguments against precipitant rejection of a nuclear strategy in Europe, however, it also is the case that one of them has to stay.

The allies are unlikely to cotton to the United States's renunciation of strategic coupling. However, the allies, and most particularly West Germany, seem even less likely to muster the political will on which Bundy and associates would rely for an expensive conventional build up. Most Europeans agree that some NATO upgrading remains desirable. Such an effort at upgrading would symbolize a continuing Western political concert. It would warn that alliance disarray has not yet proceeded all the way to the point of dissolution, and, therefore, that the Soviet Union may not misbehave with impunity. Nevertheless, the list of politically salable purposes among European electorates would not include the objective of building an impregnable conventional rampart where the nuclear wall formerly stood.

Not to put too fine a point on the matter, a promise by the Europeans to pay for a major increase in their defense posture would seem no more credible than is the offer by the United States to bring holocaust on itself as a way of ensuring the security of Europe. The alliancewide conventional upgrading is no more credible than is indefinite strategic coupling. Given the Europeans' record of burden shirking, if Bundy and his collaborators really propose that the allies bear major burdens in a major conventional upgrading, then they may have presented a formula for nuclear abnegation with conventional impotence.

NATO at an Impasse

The unreliability of alliancewide financial promises, compounded by the continuing unacceptability of West Germany's acquisition of the weapon that is best trusted for frontal deterrence, have brought NATO force planning to an impasse. Frontal deterrence in Europe cannot be restored by substituting upgraded conventional forces for the nuclear components—not, at least, if one wants a reasonably affordable posture on the central front. Nor can the United States simply throw its hands up and retrench, because West Germany's need for continuing military patronage has not diminished. If the central front is to be stabilized by an adequate conventional/nuclear force, the United States will have to go on providing at least the nuclear element in it—which, of course, brings the analysis right back to the problem of eroding credibility, as demands within the United States to deliver U.S. cities from their current hostage status inexorably weaken the reliability of the nation's willingness to fulfill a promise of continued strategic coupling.

A battlefield nuclear strategy seems to offer the only feasible outlet from the NATO impasse—provided, of course, that such a strategy can be sold to West Germany without a simultaneous reaffirmation of strategic coupling. Indeed, the position of the Federal Republic will be as crucial in the effort to reensure the NATO posture as it was in the original design of extended nuclear deterrence. West Germany, not the Soviet Union, still controls the problem of a stable Europe—certainly from the political standpoint, and probably in strategic terms as well. West Germany, not NATO, should be the focus of the United States's concern on the Continent.

West German Stakes—and Risks—in NATO

In West Germany's case, the reasons for probable burden shirking during a conventional build up have to do not only with its singular— and now habitual—reliance on the nuclear threat. They have to do not only with perceptions of the economic distress that afflicts the Federal Republic: The Germans argue that they cannot afford to fund a costly conventional build up.[11] The reasons also have to do with West Germany's view of the equities within the alliance. Because the Federal Republic probably will provide the battlefield, someone else should provide most of the battle units.

Under the traditional theory of the proper division of labor within the alliance, NATO's forces should be drawn in accordance with the participant countries' resources and their respective comparative advantages.[12] While the poor but numerous Europeans were rebuilding after World War II, U.S. allies' comparative advantage putatively lay in the provision of manpower for whatever fighting forces (as opposed to the U.S. trip-wire force) that NATO might mount. The comparative advantage of the United States lay in the provision of nuclear deterrence—made feasible by U.S. wealth and technology, made credible by the nation's visible determination to play the role of Free World leader. The conventional/nuclear division of labor, which thus broadly corresponded to the European and American shares of the common burden, gave rise first to the United States's pledge of strategic coupling and then to its mounting of a battlefield nuclear posture as low-yield weapons became available. Under the trip-wire doctrine, a thin line of U.S. troops would be stretched across the central front—not to fight a war of resistance against Soviet frontal forces, but to ensure that vital U.S. interests would be engaged by means of the shedding of American boys' blood as the invaders rushed westward, thus making the nuclear retaliatory threat credible.

However, in the event of a Warsaw Pact move on the central front, the relevant division of labor today would not correspond to the conventional/nuclear distinction. Rather, it would correspond to the distinction between the United States, Britain, and France, which conceivably could expect to fight on foreign soil and West Germany, which certainly would have to fight to defend its home land.

West Germany's Geostrategic Burden

There exist three principal scenarios for war in Europe. There is, first, the scenario for the war that stays confined to the territory of the Federal

Republic. Then there is the broader war that results from the Warsaw Pact bolt from the blue followed by the sweep to the Atlantic that has long figured in NATO rhetoric. Finally, there is the all-out war that involves, in addition to the destruction of Europe, escalation to an U.S.-Soviet nuclear exchange. All of the NATO partners, except the Germans, have real incentives to keep a conflict confined to a variation of the first scenario. None, except the Germans, has an unambiguous incentive to build escalatory presumptions into NATO planning as a way of deterring any war, even one scripted to follow the first scenario, lest it become the war of the second scenario or, worse, the third scenario.

The United States has never been able to talk Britain into decommissioning the independent deterrent force that its submarine-launchable nuclear missiles represent.[13] France lays even greater stress than does Britain on doctrines of nuclear independence.[14] France also has greater strategic independence, thanks to its pulling out of an integrated NATO command and planning structure. One suspects, too, that France, remembering the humiliation of Vichy, may have something to prove about national resolve, or "la grandeur," something sufficient for French decision makers to use nuclear weapons if pushed to do so in defense of their own territory.

Thus, the political and military calculus of a war in Europe would change as soon as Warsaw Pact frontal forces, in that feared sweep to the Atlantic, crossed the Rhine. Moreover, the calculus would change abruptly irrespective of U.S. policy on first use. Whether hostilities went nuclear or not at the point of transition from the first to the second scenario would depend mainly on the heirs of DeGaulle, not on policies negotiated between Washington and Bonn. The elevated nuclear risk associated with a trespass on French territory implies a correspondingly lowered likelihood that the Soviet Union would opt for the second scenario.

Whatever the odds that a Warsaw Pact move on the central front might eventually lead to a move on France as well, West Germany has no such independence as France enjoys with respect to an attack on its eastern flank. West Germany, which would suffer the first and probably the worst in any war in Europe, bears the gravest burden within the alliance. And it bears this burden whether it does or does not make extra economic sacrifices to upgrade conventional defenses. West Germany might suppose that its current contribution of almost half of NATO's conventional capability, plus its own extraordinary and invidious exposure—partly the result of European political geography, but also partly the result of West Germany's choice (so far) against neutrality—represent an ample sacrifice on behalf of the Atlantic Community, or NATO solidarity, or whatever it is that the alliance symbolizes today.

If the whole of the nuclear and the conventional capability on the central front were stamped "Made in U.S.A.," West Germany still would perceive that it has more to lose than the United States does in a war limited to central Europe. So, unless a strategy can be devised that vastly reduces the probability that NATO and Warsaw Pact forces might try to settle underlying political differences on German terrain, West Germany would just as soon—and not unreasonably—pay relatively less for the forces that would do the fighting.

If West Germany Looks East . . .

Of course, as an alternative to spending more for conventional defenses against the Soviet Union, West Germany also could try to relieve the strains that it feels by moving to settle some of its own political differences with the Soviet Union. What might such moves imply for the continuing effort at European stabilization? What if West Germany looks east?

In attempting to answer these questions, one must remember that a German problem, even more than a Soviet problem, underlies the continuing unease in Europe. The bitter legacy of World War II is far from spent. Ever since Yalta and Potsdam, U.S.-Soviet tensions have been confounded not only with Russian and French fears of their historic tormentors, the Germans, but also with the Germans' own yearnings for greater political independence. A sublimation of these yearnings could become the most potent source of European destabilization in the foreseeable future. As Zbigniew Brzezinski has put it:

> We are witnessing something taking place in Germany which defies easy categorization, something which should not be reduced simply to the slogan "Neutralism or Pacifism." Something which is in some deeper sense a revival as well as a transmutation of more traditional German nationalism and a resurfacing of an Eastern orientation as the basic geopolitical outlook of that Central European and so crucial nation. That, of course, has very great significance for the stability and homogeneity of the Western alliance. We are witnessing in effect the dilution of the Atlantic perspective. . . .[15]

The independent nationalist aspirations that have repeatedly revealed themselves in the communist satellite countries—most recently, in Poland—mirror the intensification of the nationalist spirit in West Germany, just as they are of a piece with the Frankish aspirations that

DeGaulle symbolized in the 1950s and 1960s. These aspirations, not the political artifices of the hegemonic powers—the NATO and Warsaw Pact alliances are such artifacts—point time's arrow. These independent nationalist yearnings suggest the course of history.

If the United States reacts in a responsible and realistic way, the restive mood of West Germany can favor the promotion, over the long term, of a freer political order from the Atlantic to the Curzon Line, if not to the Urals. U.S. policies toward NATO Europe will decisively influence Soviet perceptions of the military balance and, hence, Soviet policies in Eastern Europe. A fully militarized, politically unified Atlantic alliance will cause the Soviet Union to redouble its efforts to keep the Warsaw Pact similarly unified. Obversely, the United States probably can best encourage a loosening of the Soviet lines into the satellites by means of a gradual loosening of NATO ties.

This will have to be done carefully, very carefully. The loosening of NATO ties probably will have to occur, as has the entire quest for a stable peace, through periodic and piecemeal adjustments. The Soviet Union has shown, most recently by its role in the Polish 'restabilization', just how gradual and guarded—and grudging—any loosening of its grip on Eastern Europe will be. One looks, then, for no rapid evacuation of the alien presence beyond the East-West dividing line, such as might soon justify an equal and like reaction by the United States.

If the United States were simultaneously to decouple its strategic forces and renounce its willingness to meet a frontal assault with battlefield nuclear weapons, it would abruptly forfeit much of the equity that it has built up in NATO Europe, and particularly in West Germany. The real danger to European stability would lie in a premature cession of U.S. influence over central European affairs. A wholesale withdrawal of U.S. influence could relieve West Germany of a sense of obligation. It could put West Germany, which is anxious to penetrate Eastern markets and cultivate Eastern political ties, in a swing position. From a more nearly neutralized position, it could play the superpowers against each other, especially in arms negotiations and trade agreements. Helmut Schmidt's eagerness, during the latter portion of his chancellorship, to serve as interpreter between East and West suggest that West Germany might seize on an opportunity to convert the role of partner into that of broker.

Walter Lippmann foresaw the possibility of West Germany's accession to the pivot position in a context of continuing East-West confrontation. Worse, he foresaw the possibility of the seduction of West Germany by the Soviet Union, whose control over East Germany gives it a trading stamp with enormous purchasing power in the Federal Republic.[16] Either development would betoken a qualitative change in the balance of power. Either could lead to further destabilization in Europe. And either would be far more likely to occur if the United States should let the Federal Republic slip toward political neutrality, whence it could move to who knows what subsequent course in international relations.[17]

Fortunately, West Germany would not, in the near future, happily trade its political affiliation for neutrality, let alone for the kind of security that East Germany enjoys in the clasp of the bear. The return to power in early 1983 of the pro-United States Christian Democrats underscored the commitment of the Federal Republic to NATO. Neither would U.S. interests be served if, in the future, West Germany were to reduce its unique vulnerability by veering back more sharply on the course that Ostpolitik presaged—the course of a further gradual compromising of the Federal Republic's orientation toward the West.

Because West Germany may be expected to recognize the United States's interest in holding fast to an intimate and interdependent relationship, it doubtless will think that charging a price for what it has to offer is fair. What it has to offer is what it has to withhold—continued firm encampment on the Western side. The very fact that West Germany now has it in its power to make such a choice marks perhaps the most dramatic change on the European political landscape since DeGaulle presided over the nationalist renaissance in France.

A U.S.-German Bargain

West Germany's political ascendency, then, will give force to its likely demand for a quid pro quo if it indefinitely maintains a political orientation toward the West—which also implies a posture of some military antagonism toward the East. Above all, West Germany must be expected to demand a reliable, a steadfast forward deterrent—if not a deterrent based on strategic coupling, then at least one based on a force structure that stabilizes the military balance to its satisfaction but involves little more in the way of defense outlays than West Germany became accustomed to spending while it was able to rely on the protection of a credible U.S. strategic threat.

Apparently, nothing less than a nuclear posture can meet West Germany's sometimes macabre-seeming fixation on the military danger from the East. That fixation grips West Germany's political leaders more insistently than it does the masses. It may weaken with time, as citizens of the Federal Republic translate rapidly rising antinuclear sentiments into demands on their leaders. These demands already show signs of moving some German politicians (for example, members of the left wing of the Social Democratic Party) toward open advocacy of political and military neutralization.[18] But for a while, retention of a nuclear option in some form seems necessary to serve U.S. political interests in Europe, lest West Germany feels pushed by its uncompensated military insecurities toward political wavering.

On the other side of the bargaining table, it would be reasonable for the United States to try to buy out—*buy out* is the consequential phrase—of the fully coupled relationship. Of course, it will remain in the power of U.S. officials to declare continued adherence to the policy of strategic coupling, that is, the pledging of U.S. strategic forces to the mission of frontal deterrence in Europe. It already is in the power of the U.S. electorate, however, to undercut the credibility, and hence the deterrent value, of such a policy, notwithstanding official reaffirmations. Any U.S.-German bargain that fails to achieve at least partial decoupling eventually will prove politically unstable on the U.S. side, as rising demands within the United States to deliver American cities from their exposure to nuclear peril gradually weaken the reliability of the U.S. pledge.

The Vocabulary of Decoupling

What practical steps would the United States take to signal its intention to move toward strategic decoupling? It would not precipitantly withdraw its strategic umbrella by passing a congressional resolution that declares the United States to be decoupled and then have the U.S. NATO ambassador quietly but firmly tell the allies one by one to 'flake off.' The appropriate vocabulary of the decoupling process is not that of the formal resolution or the explicit declaration. Rather, it is that of the messages the United States would communicate by gradually adjusting its force structure and weapons deployments. The aim should be to structure U.S. forces in NATO Europe so that they convey the United States's determination to give due support to U.S. allies—that is, to provide for frontal deterrence—but to do so while bringing U.S. commitments into line with the political and economic realities of the 1980s.

In the NATO area, it has been well appreciated that the United States's follow-through on plans to deploy the so-called Eurostrategic missiles from Great Britain to Sicily will give the crucial signal of U.S. strategic intentions.

The Eurostrategic Deployments

The plan to site the Eurostrategics within reach of the Soviet Union initially was viewed as a U.S. response to Chancellor Schmidt's call, in a much-publicized 1977 speech, for an answer to Soviet deployment of SS-20 intermediate-range rockets targeted on Western Europe.[19] Nuclear parity having already been achieved between the United States and the Soviet Union at the strategic level, Schmidt wanted to equalize the theater nuclear balance.

Both the Pershing II ballistic missiles and the Tomahawk-G (for ground launched) cruise missiles would be able to hit strategic targets deep in Eastern Europe. However, although both systems therefore qualify to be called Eurostrategic, they differ fundamentally in their operational capabilities. Pershing II, a three-warhead weapon, would have a six-minute trajectory from its launch sites in West Germany to targets near Moscow. These targets could include key components of the Soviet Union's radar warning network. The Pershing's serviceability for time-urgent strategic counterforce and countercontrol missions makes it a potentially destabilizing first strike weapon. For this reason, the Soviet Union has voiced especial alarm over U.S. intentions to deploy 108 of these weapons at launch sites in West Germany.[20] By contrast, the proposed Tomahawk-Gs—464 of them—would fly at near ground level, tracking their courses by sophisticated map-reading computers, but taking hours to reach their targets. The case can be made, therefore, that cruise missiles are second strike rather than first strike weapons.

Whether the intended mix of Pershing IIs and Tomahawk-Gs adds up to a preemptive or a second strike threat, the Eurostrategic deployments would signal the United States's intention to maintain the coupled relationship with NATO Europe, which is why proponents of the standard view tend to favor the deployments as a signal of unity within the Atlantic Community.[21] Central to the position of these supporters of community is the concept of the seamless web: the concept of a continuum of nuclear capabilities, from short-range battlefield weapons all the way up to the intercontinental striking forces. The seamlessness of the nuclear web becomes a metaphor for the solidarity of the Atlantic Community. The U.S. military posture gives the same message to Europe—and the Soviet Union—that U.S. political assurances do.

President Reagan supported the Eurostrategics on the basis of this seamless web doctrine.[22] However, he also opened the door to cancellation of the U.S. deployments if the Soviet Union would dismantle its European-based SS-3s, SS-4s, and mobile three-warhead SS-20s. The president offered his so-called zero-zero proposal as a way of making good on the NATO ministers' two-track decision of December 20, 1979. With this decision, the United States pledged to negotiate with the Soviet Union for reductions in the numbers of intermediate-range missile launchers that both sides had planned for deployment in

Europe. The United States would barrel ahead with the development of its new Eurostrategic weapons (the first track) while trying to persuade the Soviet Union to draw down its SS-20s (the second track), so as to obviate any need for the deployment of U.S. Pershings and Tomahawks when they became operational.

Political and Strategic Uncertainties

As a result of the two-track decision and the continuing Geneva negotiations to which it led, the plans for Eurostrategic missile emplacements became clouded by political uncertainties. U.S. and Soviet leaders alike began to bid for "the hearts and minds of Europe." At the same time, second thoughts about the wisdom of deploying a new generation of nuclear weapons surfaced on the Continent and in England.[23] As the antinuclear movement gained steam across Europe, the Soviet Union tried to exploit pacifist sentiments and thereby split the alliance. By manipulating the same sentiments, the United States sought to prove itself to be the leader in the party of peace. Proposals from both superpowers for cutbacks and cancellations in planned Eurostrategic deployments became the coinage in a bidding war, with European public opinion as the stake in the contest.

Then, in early 1983, the year of the first planned U.S. Eurostrategic deployments, the victory of the Christian Democrat Helmut Kohl in the West German general elections seemed to presage a return, after thirteen years of the Ostpolitik of Willy Brandt and Helmut Schmidt, to the more Western-oriented policies of the 1950s and 1960s. Kohl's victory having demonstrated West Germany's loyalty to the U.S. planners' idea of a militarily upgraded alliance, the West Germans joined other European leaders in persuading President Reagan to drop his unsalable zero-zero proposal. In its place, the president offered an interim proposal that would provide for U.S. deployment of some Eurostrategics and Soviet dismantling of some SS-20s. The Soviet Union duly rejected the new Reagan overture, as they had rejected zero-zero—and just as the United States had rejected various plans that the Soviet Union put forward—leaving movement toward a political solution to the Eurostrategic problem at an impasse.

To the political uncertainties regarding the unacceptability of each side's negotiating proposals to the other, the nuclear theologians added a temporary nebula of strategic uncertainty. Would the deployments, if they did occur, have the expected effect of confirming a coupled relationship? Or would they have precisely the opposite effect of decoupling U.S. central forces from the European theater? Costly nuclear systems of U.S. manufacture and under U.S. control, but based in Europe, would cover targets in the Soviet home land. These forces could pick up the retaliatory mission of the U.S.-based forces. Why would the United States risk a Soviet counterstrike on U.S. cities by committing its strategic nuclear forces to a mission that could be covered by midrange missiles based in Great Britain, Italy, the Low Countries, and West Germany? With the Eurostrategics in place, the credibility of strategic coupling would be irreversibly damaged if not disavowed. Thus, a Eurostrategic plan that had been justified in the late 1970s as a means of ensuring strategic coupling by way of the seamless web became transmuted, by inference and interpretation, into a vehicle of strategic decoupling.

It was a Soviet spokesman, not Western thinkers, who settled the uncertainty over the strategic effect of any deployments. In a March 16, 1983, interview with Western journalists, Soviet Marshall N.V. Ogarkov emphasized that any U.S. use of Eurostrategic missiles in the course of a war between NATO and the Warsaw Pact would draw forth a retaliatory response against the United States as well as against European targets.[24] In other words, the Soviet Union would interpret the deployments as a confirmation of strategic coupling.

Unfortunately, that would be precisely the opposite of the signal that the United States should want, in the long run, to give. U.S. interests lie in signaling an intent to recognize domestic and international political realities by moving toward strategic decoupling. At the theater level, as at the level of the direct confrontation between superpowers, U.S. interests also lie in signaling a determination to limit a war—even a nuclear war—if one should come. By withholding deployments, the United States would signal its intent to observe a limit on the use of battlefield nuclear weapons—that is, an intent not to escalate from a frontal war to the level of midrange missile strikes against targets deep in Eastern Europe. U.S. interest in strategic decoupling implies a determination to interrupt the pathways that could lead from a frontal conflict in mid-Europe to a direct superpower conflict. The use—or even the emplacement—of Eurostrategics could hardly help but obscure the buffer that the United States should be trying to interpose between frontal and total war.

Buffering against Escalation

The term *buffer* is used here in the broadest possible way, to refer to any boundary or principle of discrimination that can help combatants recognize discrete regimes of warfare. Some buffers have great physical clarity. The most familiar buffer, the conventional/nuclear firebreak, has such distinctness. Other buffers are less precise. They mark zones of transition on a contiuum, rather than unambiguous break points. The counterforce-countervalue dichotomy is of such description. That is, that dichotomy is not truly dichotomous, although, even as an unprecise category of strategic thought, the concept of counterforce has usefulness as a guide to targeting discrimination.

Those who simply deny that a nuclear war can ever be controlled tend to frame the simplest possible system of buffers—the system that consists of but a single boundary between limitable (read: conventional) war and armageddon. To cross that one boundary is to go all the way. Thus, according to Bundy and his co-authors, "The one clearly definable firebreak against the worldwide disaster of general nuclear war is the one that stands between all other kinds of conflict and any use whatsoever of nuclear weapons."[25] The thought has become familiar to the point of banality, but it is not on that account necessarily true. The buffer that most needs to be observed when thinking about war in Europe may not correspond to the qualitative firebreak between conventional and nuclear weapons.

The aim of western policy since World War II has been to keep Warsaw Pact forces from breaching the political boundary between East and West. It has hitherto been the purpose of U.S. nuclear weapons to deter aggression, not just to deter the Soviet Union's use of nuclear weapons to carry out the aggression. The inviolability of the geographic border between a would-be aggressor and an intended victim may still take priority over the inviolability of the conventional/nuclear firebreak. Actually, the importance of the conventional/nuclear firebreak stems mainly from the hypothesis that a determination not to go nuclear at all might be the only way to ensure that a nuclear frontal war will not escalate to an all-out superpower exchange. However, the hypothesis of inevitable escalation can become a self-fulfilling prophecy, particularly if the buffers against further jumps have been permitted to fall into disrepair, or if they have slipped from notice as a consequence of intellectually arrogant assertions that they do not exist.

To eliminate a potential fire-free zone on the nuclear spectrum by filling it with weapons systems, such as Eurostrategic missiles, whose very existence would invite escalation, is to miss the best opportunity for developing a system of buffers. It is this caveat that probably proves decisive against the Pershing II and Tomahawk-G deployments.

The Eurostrategic emplacements should be cancelled—particularly if the United States wants to retain a battlefield first-use option, because retention of that option would presuppose efforts to widen the buffers against escalation after the first nuclear shots have been fired. The

Eurostrategic plan works in exactly the wrong direction: toward greater skepticism about the possibility of escalation proofing, because the deployments would tend to eliminate the buffer that the withholding of midrange weapons could interpose between strategic and battlefield uses of nuclear weapons. This does necessarily argue against the production and stockpiling of new Pershing II and Tomahawk-G missiles. Deployments, however, should be withheld, certainly during Soviet good behavior, as a way to keep the buffers against conflict instability clearer than they otherwise would be.

A Negotiating Position

With a decision to withhold having been made on political grounds (the importance of moving toward strategic decoupling) and on strategic grounds (the importance of opening a buffer zone on the spectrum of violence), the United States could begin seriously to consider the best offer that the Soviet Union has yet laid on the table in the Geneva two-track negotiations: General Secretary Andropov's proposal for a cutback of Soviet midrange rocket launchers to some 161 missiles west of the Urals, in exchange for the United States's cancellation of the proposed deployments of Pershing II and Tomahawk-G missiles.[26] Andropov subsequently sweetened the offer by hinting at the Soviet Union's willingness to negotiate toward parity in NATO-Warsaw Pact warheads, rather than just parity in launcher numbers.

To be more than just a ploy, the Andropov plan would have to provide for the destruction of some 440 Soviet intermediate-range rockets, not their mere removal to trans-Urals sites within reach of NATO Europe or to sites in far Siberia, where they would menace Japan. With this stipulation, the number of Soviet rockets left to target NATO Europe would match the number of British and French missiles targeted against Eastern Europe. The symbolism of this equivalence could hardly be more obvious: British and French—but no U.S.—missiles in Western Europe, with Soviet cutbacks to establish a kind of Eurostrategic nuclear balance in the cis-Urals region. The superpowers would simultaneously target intercontinental forces against each other. The arrangement clearly would envision the possibility of, say, Franco-Soviet or U.S.-Soviet nuclear exchanges in which French involvement need not necessarily drag the United States into war, or vice versa. It is the symbolism of decoupling.

Acceptance of the 161-161 deal would result in independent strategic positions for some European countries, Britain and France. Their independent strategic positions would be analogous to the independent trading postures that almost all European countries have adopted. Of course, the allies would gain markets in Eastern Europe by going their own ways in matters of trade. In the matter of security, however, the allies ostensibly can only lose if the United States should cut a deal with the Soviet Union to withdraw the strategic mantle that now spreads the nuclear risk—alas, without equitably spreading the costs—of collective security.

It is the part of statecraft to foresee the inevitable and to extract some political gain from wasting assets while they can still generate real dividends. The "common heritage" of the Atlantic Community is becoming a wasting asset. As changes in the U.S. political base undermine the credibility of the U.S. pledge, Europe should recognize that it may be left with neither a credible U.S. strategic umbrella nor a steadfast forward defense, unless it joins with the United States in rescuing the one part of the NATO posture that remains rescuable. The allies' agreement to a long-term U.S. move toward strategic decoupling would represent a bargaining chip they could use to gain a satisfactory U.S. contribution to a front-line defense with a battlefield nuclear option.

Battlefield Nuclear Use

With every effort having been made to rend the seamless web—or, equivalently, to interrupt the escalatory pathway from frontal war to all-out war, or to interpose a buffer at a critical jump point in the network of threats—the United States would be able to consult with its West German partners on the future policy governing battlefield nuclear initiation.

The concept of a U.S.-German bargain need not be taken too literally. The idea merely suggests that, as part of the continuing give-and-take among members of the alliance, the two most critically committed powers must gradually work toward the new special strategy without which NATO, already slipping into political disarray, probably cannot be rescued from strategic disarray.

With the process of strategic decoupling understood on all sides to be going forward apace, the new strategy would have to provide for effective frontal deterrence on the ground in Europe. It perhaps merits emphasis that the process of decoupling in and of itself would produce a special strategy for Europe, because then the U.S. posture for frontal deterrence would have to work on its own, that is, not as a by-product of a U.S. strategic retaliatory threat. Furthermore, the elimination of Pershing II and Tomahawk-G missiles from the picture would help to convert the special strategy for Europe—at least so far as the United States's NATO commitment is concerned—from a strategy with a major retaliatory component to one that has the potential for stressing nuclear resistance. The kinds of nuclear arms that the United States maintains near the central front—short-range artillery versus farther-reaching tactical air forces; low-yield versus medium-yield warheads—will determine, in large measure, how closely the U.S. posture approximates the one needed for a special strategy of nuclear resistance.

Many critics of the current NATO posture—and not just the proponents of no first use, either—have raised doubts about allied forces' ability to meet the feared frontal attack without being drawn willy-nilly into a theater nuclear war. Indeed, it is true that the disposition of U.S. short-range nuclear forces along the central front—some 6,000 battlefield nuclear weapons, mostly in known locations all over West Germany and the Low Countries—creates an incentive to use them or lose them in the event of a frontal push by the enemy. It makes for a tense situation at best and, at worst, for a downright unstable one.

A move to defuse tensions on the central front could be made by removing U.S. tactical nuclear warheads altogether—or, at least, as in a plan advanced by Senator Sam Nunn, by drawing their numbers down and, with respect to those that remain, offering a conditional pledge of no first use.[27] In the Nunn plan, a program of conventional upgrading would be set in motion. Negotiations for mutual reductions in NATO and Warsaw Pact nuclear warhead numbers would then be started. As a further element in the Nunn plan, NATO's no-first-use pledge would be abrogated only in response to the Warsaw Pact's assembly of large concentrations of conventional ground forces—especially armored forces. Of course, such an understanding would merely codify tactics that commanders on both sides already understand, because nuclear initiation makes military sense only when extraordinarily dense firepower must be directed against massed enemy forces.

On the other hand, when planners can reasonably anticipate that an assault would take the form of massed armored assaults—which the Red Army manuals prescribe for a frontal attack—then the nuclear threat makes a great deal of sense indeed. Massed assaults can, of course, refer to true bolt-from-the-blue attacks by enemy forces in echelon. The probabilistic imagery of the threat, however, suggests that massed assaults most likely would occur after a more localized war had turned against the Soviet Union, which thereupon—in a kind of desperation brought on by a general deterioration of the Party's domestic position—might release its frontal forces in a grab for territory to be used when bargaining for a truce. This desperation element has, in the most credible version of the threat, multifold implications. It implies, first of all, that the scenario of the massed frontal attack does not occur at the beginning of a probable chain of events, but well along such a sequence. The probabilistic imagery heightens the sense of unlikelihood that attaches to this scenario, which further implies that the prudent course would involve choice of the less rather than the more expensive posture to defend against it. On a rational economic basis, the case for a nuclear rather than a conventional defense on NATO's central front becomes stronger as the need to use it becomes less likely.

On the other hand, in the heat of actual warfare, the desperation element as a factor in Soviet decision making raises the danger of hasty or irrational moves—a possibility that never can be eliminated altogether, but one that perhaps can be more effectively dampened by an awareness on both sides that the United States would use the most dramatic and decisive means at its disposal to block a Warsaw Pact frontal move.

A New Deterrent Formula, a New Battlefield Doctrine

Use of battlefield nuclear weapons to meet just those enemy moves— massed frontal moves—for which nuclear weapons have the comparative advantage implies a change in the relationship between ingredients 1 and 2 in the accepted formula for extended deterrence (see chapter 2's section on central and extended deterrence). In that formula, conventional forces and battlefield nuclear weapons are ticketed for sequential use to counter an enemy move. Even if Warsaw Pact forces should launch a major offensive in Europe, the presumed initial response would be conventional (ingredient 1), with battlefield nuclear weapons (ingredient 2) held for back-up use. The more effective the conventional defenses can be made, the higher the threshold that can be set for nuclear initiation.

By contrast, nuclear frontal deterrence implies early and decisive use of battlefield warheads in the event of an enemy frontal move— just as it implies the withholding of a battlefield nuclear response to less-than-frontal contingencies, even if those contingencies should begin to turn against the United States because of a failure of U.S. conventional forces. It almost goes without saying that this strategy further implies the need to deploy conventional forces with exceedingly high probabilities of meeting less-than-frontal moves successfully. Plainly, the chances of meeting this requirement depend on suitable delimitation of the challenges with which the conventional forces may be asked to deal—the key point being that the containment of massed assaults seems to lie beyond the bounds of such suitable delimitation.

In other words, instead of being driven by tactical necessity to use nuclear weapons if the Soviet Union should push it to the fateful decision, the United States probably should be prepared to use them as the weapons of choice rather than of desperation—on the premise that such willingness represents today, as it has in the past, the United States's best chance to deter the Soviet frontal push from happening in the first place. As has been emphasized already, battlefield nuclear weapons should be used, to the extent possible, in a resistive rather than a retaliatory mode by confining their use at the line of aggression to within as narrow a band along a forward edge of the battle area (FEBA) as can be maintained.

Can a special strategy be devised for NATO's central front that does not imply the deployment of Eurostrategic weapons or otherwise implicitly recouple the forward segment of the U.S. nuclear posture (that is, the frontal deterrent) to the central segment (the primary deterrent), one that does not carry too high a threat, if used, of uncontrollable escalation—that is, one that would replace the imagery of holocaust with an imagery of limits and, at the same time, would not mock military or political good sense?

A plan that meets these criteria might involve the retention, at high alert in a forward posture, of short-range, low-yield weapons, including enhanced radiation warheads, to be governed by a doctrine of early first use. The term *early* perhaps is the crucial modifier, and also the one most at odds with the familiar notions of threshold raising and of a pause before nuclear initiation. Early use implies that nuclear warheads would be employed, if at all, only while the forward edge of the battle area remained a relatively narrow, clearly demarcated front. Analysts at the Stockholm International Peace Research Institute—hardly a hotbed of hawkish strategic ideas—have estimated that one thousand enhanced radiation weapons might be needed to stop a major tank attack.[28] No one suggests that neutron warhead explosions in such numbers would be other than a catastrophe for those in the area of the battle. At the same time, it is worth noting that a properly modified order of battle on the central front could consist of a forward nuclear line with far fewer systems than the currently deployed inventory represents.

This nuclear forward defense posture also would incorporate the principle of the best shot, albeit in a form that differs from the similar principle implied by Bundy and his collaborators. Under an early first-use strategy, NATO political decision makers would have to be prepared to make a quick decision regarding the allies' best shot: conventional only, or—in the event of frontal aggression—use of nuclear weapons. The best shot having been taken, it then would be the U.S.

policy to observe the buffers against further escalation. No additional nuclear weapons would be brought up to the forward edge should the front fail to hold. No U.S.-controlled Eurostrategic missiles would be waiting for the release order that could end up recoupling the conflict to the central forces.

U.S. Conventional Forces

Reservation of the conventional forces for the limited mission of resisting limited (as opposed to frontal) incursions also should hint at the proper sizing, equipping, and posturing of U.S. nonnuclear units in Europe.

Unfortunately, for some time there has been no consensus as to the best way of ordering U.S. conventional forces on the central front. Should the United States upgrade its units with the next generation of high technology systems or equip them with old-fashioned rifles, with tanks that have no fancy "bells and whistles," and with other easy-to-maintain weapons?[29] Should the United States maintain the forward positional posture that the Europeans generally have preferred or switch to more dynamic, maneuverable tactics, as members of the so-called Military Reform Caucus of the U.S. Congress recently have begun to advocate?[30]

The Case against High Technology

The most promising high technology conventional systems have both "legs" and "smarts." They have mobility and range (their legs). They have computerized sensors and controls (their smarts). In a frontal war between NATO and the Warsaw Pact, these systems' sophisticated guidance equipment would permit firepower to be directed against Warsaw Pact tank concentrations miles behind the FEBA, as well as against massed armored forces at the front. U.S. battlefield controllers, orbiting over West Germany in special airplanes, could use radar to see where Warsaw Pact commanders were positioning their back-up armored forces. They then would use unjammable radio signals to guide multiple-warhead rockets to the area of the enemy concentrations. The individual warheads would then detach. Using infrared or heat-seeking sensors, these individual warheads would identify enemy tanks and destroy them one by one. Thus, proponents of these high technology systems envision that they would be used to knock out Warsaw Pact rear-echelon forces so as to leave the attacking force as a mere drag-onhead without a body.[31]

The case for adopting these high technology systems hinges on the desirability of adopting a particular war-waging strategy in Europe. That strategy would require the United States to take the battle far into enemy territory by hitting his combat reserves and supply units. However, the decision to rely on so-called second-echelon attack strat-egies requires a judgment: Does having an alternative to early first use of nuclear warheads justify a high technology conventional strategy that would tend to expand a war in Europe by requiring the United States to strike far behind enemy lines? The answer is, arguably, no.

The first move in a European war presumably would not be the United States's—not even if it rather than the invaders made first use of nuclear weapons. First move is different from first use. Given an enemy first move, however, the aim of U.S. military resistance, whether nuclear or conventional, should be to stop the attacker at the line of aggression. It should not be to retaliate. It should not be to answer aggression with strikes far behind the violated borders, particularly if (as in Eastern Europe) there dwell beyond those borders people who never freely chose to become satellites of the Soviet Union. A strategy of nuclear resistance that could reasonably be expected to stop a frontal assault within a narrow FEBA must be preferred to a strategy of con-ventional counterattacks that would broaden the belt of destruction.

Second-echelon systems imply a mode of resistance that is excessive to the point of being retaliatory. As such, use of these systems would provoke retaliation in return. After all, the brains and muscles of the smart U.S. conventional systems would be represented by control cen-ters and launch sites in the second- and third-echelon units of friendly forces. They would be deployed in the interior of West Germany to hit rear-echelon targets in the interior of East Germany, Czechoslo-vakia, and perhaps even Austria, Hungary, or Poland. In other words, U.S. deployment of these high technology systems would invite deep preemptive strikes by the frontal air forces of the enemy. This scenario easily could read like the script for a replay of World War II—a script that also might end in one side or the other's going nuclear to cap the culminating violence.

There are no riskless strategies. The adoption of any posture can only mean that the odds seem to favor—they can never ensure—a particular approach, whether nuclear or conventional. On balance, it seems better to use battlefield nuclear warheads at the outset of a frontal move by Warsaw Pact forces. It seems better to try to end a war sooner rather than later, and while less rather than more ground has been made a casualty zone.

Fortunately, the United States already has an array of relatively short-range nuclear cannons in central Europe, weapons that should be capable of stopping a massed armored assault within a narrow FEBA. This force includes almost two thousand M-109 and M-110 atomic howitzers with ranges of twenty kilometers or less and yields of fewer than two kilotons per round. These and kindred weapons—not a new generation of longer-range conventional systems—should continue to serve as the mainstay of the U.S. forward posture.[32]

Does this mean that the United States can dispense altogether with nonnuclear forces—just forget about the much-discussed conventional build up in NATO, and maybe even bring most of the troops back home? Not at all. The United States needs both battlefield nuclear and conventional capabilities in Europe. However, it probably does not need them in a mix designed primarily to raise the threshold of nuclear initiation—that is, with the idea of first trying to win a conventional frontal war while reserving the option of vertical escalation to a nuclear war if conventional resistance should fail.

Instead, conventional forces should be used only to meet a Warsaw Pact move that remains below the level of a frontal attack, and the conventional forces should be so equipped and deployed that they would have an exceedingly high probability of containing the enemy move. One would not want an enemy feint or a border incident to elicit a nuclear response for want of a conventional capability to stop a local probe. The United States probably could have forces with the requisite capability, even if it cut U.S. troop commitments well beneath the current level of 300,000—provided that the troops are equipped and deployed for the mission of local, as opposed to frontal, deterrence.

The Case against Maneuver

Tactical, geostrategic, and political considerations all suggest that the conventional as well as the nuclear resistive posture should be anchored to forward defense positions, rather than based on the maneuverable defense-in-depth strategy that has attracted partisans in recent years.

Under the tactical concept proposed by some advisers of the congressional Military Reform Caucus, lightweight tanks and mobile artillery units would be spread over West Germany.[33] Instead of trying to stop a Warsaw Pact assault at the front line—which the advocates of a maneuverable defense fear would become a brittle forward wall—U.S. mobile forces would cut the enemy to pieces in a series of tactically daring, decentralized battles. Maneuverable defense risks catastrophic defeats on the chance that superior generalship and mobility would pull off the famous victory in the field. The champions of mobility cite Hannibal, Saladin, and Stonewall Jackson as examples. This tactical concept evokes the imagery of fluid, opportunistic guerrilla warfare, but warfare played out at the level of frontal combat across central Europe.

Unfortunately, the West Germans—who know a little bit about panzer tactics—reject maneuver warfare even more adamantly than they reject no first use.[34] No first use, they fear, would increase the likelihood of war by weakening the deterrent. Then, should war come in Europe, the strategy of maneuver—like the second-echelon attack strategy—would make the Federal Republic one big military exercise ground.

Apart from the political unacceptability of a free wheeling battlefield strategy that could turn the whole of West Germany into a war zone, there are tactical and economic reasons for rejecting a strategy of maneuver. The tactical advantage in conventional warfare increasingly lies with defenders who are equipped with precision-guided bazooka-type antitank weapons and who can fire them from behind protected fortifications.[35] Positional defenses also are cheaper. It costs much less to build artificial breastworks and hedgerows than it does to field armored divisions, even if the armor consists of relatively simple light tanks.[36] It costs less, too, for the United States to manufacture precision-guided munitions (PGMs) than it does for the economically troubled Soviet-bloc countries to build the tanks that PGMs can make vulnerable. Indeed, it is in support of front-line defenders, not in deep-penetration attacks, that smart weapons—in the form of PGMs—show the real promise of conventional high technology.[37]

Perhaps the decisive argument against the strategy of maneuver rests on the fact that a positional posture on the central front sends a stabilizing signal to the Soviet Union and its satellite leaders, precisely because it implies defensive planning. A highly maneuverable force, which inherently possesses dual offensive-defensive capabilities, or second-echelon weapons deployments, which telegraph an intent to launch deep-penetration strikes, have more threatening implications. If the aim of nuclear resistance to a Warsaw Pact frontal move is to stop the attack with a decisive but also a confined and restrained response, the aim of conventional resistance should be to stop a low-level incursion by means that would tend to limit a war to the locale of the attack.

A Decoupled Forward Deterrent

The preceeding survey of the situation on NATO's central front suggests a more or less clear-cut outline of U.S. force needs there: a somewhat smaller troop commitment than is currently maintained, but one dug in at the far border of West Germany rather than spread out in depth across the Federal Republic; a force conventionally equipped for high-confidence resistance of low-level Warsaw Pact moves at the line of aggression, rather than for second-echelon responses to frontal attacks; and a force known to be ready for immediate nuclear resistance using short-range atomic warheads in the event of a frontal attack.

The U.S. conventional posture should be such that gives the United States a very good chance of containing a move of less-than-frontal proportions. Indeed, it should be sufficiently solid to convince Warsaw Pact decision makers that no move of less-than-frontal proportions would be likely to overrun U.S. conventional defenses. For the same reason, U.S. battlefield nuclear capabilities and strategic intentions—early first use in a resistive mode, using short-range nuclear artillery within a geographically limited FEBA—also should be clear enough to convince Warsaw Pact decision makers that escalation to a frontal invasion would be an equally dangerous course of action.

The critical components of a force structure that might meet these criteria—and their departures from the force structures that would effect currently planned changes and no first use—appear in table 5–1.

Corollary to a strategy that would seek to reestablish an imagery of limits would be steps to close the escalatory pathway that the doctrine of strategic coupling could otherwise open up in the event of a war on NATO's central front. A survey of the options that are available to the United States and the NATO allies suggests that no first use with continued strategic coupling is, in the end, no deal at all: The needed conventional build up will not occur. The pledge of U.S. "lives, fortune, and sacred honor" to shield Europe—and, for that matter, Japan—will not be believed indefinitely. Yet continued coupling while retaining a battlefield nuclear option scarcely has more credibility than does no first use with continued coupling, particularly if one assumes that battlefield first use would almost inevitably trigger the escalatory sequence that can culminate in a superpower exchange. The proponents of no first use, of course, typically begin their argument by making precisely this assumption.

On the other hand, gradual decoupling while retaining a nuclear order of battle on the NATO front line may be the best deal that the allies are likely to get.

And if the allies want a different deal . . . well, what have they to offer in return? In order to frame an answer to this question, one must move to a different plane of analysis, a plane that puts military strategy in the larger context of political and economic policy.

Table 5–1
Critical Components of U.S. NATO Force Structure under
Alternative Strategies

	Alternative 1: Flexible Response		Alternative 2: Conventional Build Up, No First Use	Alternative 3: Forward Posture, Early First Use
	Current Level	Late 1980s- Early 1990s		
Nuclear missiles, artillery				
Pershing II	–	108	–	–
Tomahawk-G	–	464	–	–
Honest John	60	–	–	–
Lance	90	120	120	–
M-109 gun	1,455	1,455	1,000	1,500
M-110 gun	390	390	300	400
Nuclear Ordnance				
Warheads in Europe	6,000	6,000	2,000	4,000
Of which Neutron	–	–	–	2,500
Army-Marine divisions				
Active				
Dedicated to NATO	19	20	22	18
Based in Europe	14	15	17	10
Also dedicated to	5	6	6	3
RDJTF[a]	2-½	2-½	2-½	–
Reserve	9	11	13	9
Air Force-Marine tactical aircraft				
Active wings	27	33	35	24
Dedicated to NATO	19	23	25	17
Also dedicated to				
RDJTF	3	4	4	–
Reserve	13	15	17	13
Other equipment and supplies				
Armored warfare				
M-1 tanks	600	7,058	8,058	3,000
M-60 tanks	3,400	3,400	4,400	3,400
Other tanks	8,000	6,000	8,000	4,000
Antitank				
Unimproved TOW	100,000	50,000	50,000	–
Adv Antitank	25,000	75,000	150,000	200,000
Suppt, Sustain'ty				
Prepos div sets	4-⅓	6-⅓	8-⅓	4-⅓
Reserve stocks, days	45	69-90	90	45

Source: Author's estimates adapted from *U.S. Military Posture for FY 1982* (Washington, D.C.: U.S. Government Printing Office, 1981), 44-45, 83-84; Caspar Weinberger, *Annual Report to Congress for FY 1983* (Washington, D.C.: U.S. Department of Defense, 1982), III-5-9; Earl Ravenal, "The Case for Withdrawal of Our Forces," *The New York Times Magazine,* 6 March 1983, 60; "Do You Sincerely Want to be Nonnuclear," *Economist* 30 (July 31, 1982):31; Barry Blechman and Mark Moore, "A Nuclear-Weapon-Free Zone in Europe," *Scientific American* 37 (April, 1983):39.

[a]RDJTF: Rapid Deployment Joint Task Force.

To begin with, the allies could bid for a measure of continued U.S. strategic patronage by adopting more forthcoming trade and tariff policies. In the jargon of contemporary foreign policy analysis, they could enter into negotiations aimed at relinking the regime of international economic policy to the regime of collective security. They could make it clear that a greater willingness by the United States to bear the main burden of providing the Free World's security forces—to include some level of reaffirmation for the extended strategic nuclear pledge—would be met with a greater willingness by U.S. allies to cooperate in restoring an open international economy. A move toward relinking would have the further desirable effect of shifting U.S. policy from the ideological to the economic orientation, thereby underscoring that the active principle of U.S. foreign policy in the 1980s will be to reopen international trade lines and restart the engines of global growth.

Thus, a move toward relinking brings three notions into play: a reorientation of U.S. foreign policy, in line with the increasing sensitivity of domestic welfare to international economic conditions; a rethinking of U.S. alliance relationships—not only with Western Europe but throughout the old arc of containment around the Eurasian rim land from NATO's central front to Japan and Korea; and a revision of U.S. overseas military posture in order to promote an open, growing international economy. It turns out that what the United States can best do toward this end—indeed, what it must do in order to restore the liberal vision—is to restore the system of local deterrence where it has fallen most greviously into disrepair: around the Asian Main.

6 Local Deterrence in Asia

At the far eastern extreme of the Asian Main, and perhaps at the apex of future U.S. political-economic concerns, stands Japan, the United States's largest trading partner and—even after due note has been taken of the power potential of the People's Republic—the key to U.S. Asian policy.[1]

Militarily, the threat of a Soviet-inspired invasion (probably from the Korean peninsula) seems to trouble the Japanese less than does the possibility of an air attack from the Asian mainland or a naval blockade by the new Minsk-class carriers with which the Soviet Union now patrols the waters around Japan.[2] The primary threats, however, are not military at all. The primary threats to Japanese independence and security are suggested by the politically intimidative displays of the Soviet Union's augmented Pacific naval forces. They are in the nature of an Asian version of the phenomenon that, in Europe, is called finlandization. Given the Soviet Union's augmented abilities to display force in the waters around Japan, the United States's Asian allies may face a choice between yielding (at least in part) to future Soviet brandishments or restoring the Asian power balance (at least to an extent) by independent military build ups—or, and this is the alternative that they themselves seem to prefer, by looking for the reassurance of a U.S. restoration in Northeast Asia.

Japanese remilitarizaton to fill a vacuum left by U.S. withdrawal would be as unsettling to the People's Republic of China, the Philippines, and the Soviet Union as German remilitarization would be to France and the Warsaw Pact nations.[3] The situation of the Japanese resembles that of the Germans in other ways as well: in the recency of these people's Western political affiliations; in their enormous national energies and technological sophistication; and in their habitual dependency on the U.S. strategic nuclear pledge.

Hasty decoupling from Japan, a nonnuclear power that the United States wants to keep nonnuclear, would be destabilizing. On the other hand, it is not clear that the Japanese need a perpetual U.S. strategic nuclear pledge of doubtful credibility. The more credible military menaces come first from the sea, secondarily from the air, and only tertiarily from Soviet or North Korean (or Chinese?) ground forces. What the Japanese need—and want—is an augmented U.S. naval presence in the Western Pacific to offset the Soviet build up at Petropavlovsk and Vladivostok. Secondarily, they need an upgraded air defense against the new Backfire-class Soviet bomber and a diplomatic offensive that convinces the Soviet Union to reduce the number of Siberian-based SS-20 rockets within reach of Japan. Only after naval and air defense requirements have been satisfied would the Japanese situation call for further investments in a forward line of ground forces counterposed against Soviet proxy forces on the Korean peninsula.

The pattern of emphases for Japanese security—naval, then air defense, and only then ground forces equipped to fight frontal wars— persists around the whole Asian Main. Moving clockwise on the map from Northeast Asia, the need for a strengthened naval presence re- mains pronounced in the waters south of Japan and becomes even more pronounced west of the Malacca Strait, that is, across the Indian Ocean from Southeast Asia to the Middle East.

Like their northern neighbors Japan and South Korea, the trio of Taiwan, Hong Kong, and Singapore have developed as global trading posts. As any U.S. citizen who uses computer chips—or, for that mat- ter, who wears clothes—must be aware, the U.S. economy has become interdependent with these countries'. Because their economies depend on safe seaborne commerce, so—to an unprecedented degree—does the United States's. Similarly, the development hopes of the Indone- sians and Malaysians are pinned on the ability of the industrial countries to expand the demand for raw resources from Southeast Asia and on these ASEAN countries' ability to supply them reliably.[4] By way of the Strait of Malacca, which carries virtually all of the tanker traffic from the Persian Gulf to Northeast Asia, the network of interdepen- dencies thence stretches across to Southwest Asia. The disruption of the Persian Gulf oil flow in 1973–74, and the consequences of the Arab prices hikes of 1979–80, suggest the dependency of the whole Free World's economic hopes on secure supply lines across the Indian Ocean and up around the Malay Peninsula to the Philippines, Taiwan, and Japan. Nor is this to mention the sensitivity of long-term Indian, Chinese, and other Third World country development hopes to the availability of steady supplies of needed imports.

How well equipped is the United States, both in terms of its ra- tionale for overseas commitments and its military presence abroad, to safeguard U.S. interests around the Asian Main?

The Rationale for Extended Deterrence

The United States's resolve to deter communist probes against U.S. allies in Asia as well as elsewhere traditionally has had a twofold justification. Politically, the United States has sought to stiffen its allies' abilities to resist aggression as a way of promoting the kind of international order that President Roosevelt's disciples envisioned after World War II: a Free World of secure states, with governments that would be sympathetic to Western values and able to withstand intimidation by any future would-be Hitlers or Tojos. Strategically, the United States has recognized that the first line of U.S. defense lies overseas, not along its own coast lines. "Freedom is indivisible," went the cold war slogan. Hence, the country has sought to deter any enemy push along the extended periphery, as well as at its own borders. In theory, such a push could end up toppling a whole series of dominoes, with ultimately incalculable consequences for the security and welfare of U.S. citizens.

To these traditional political and strategic underpinnings of the United States's extended military commitment, a further economic justification must be added, one that has special pertinence to U.S. interests around the Asian Main.

In an economically interdependent world, the United States has a stake in the stability of overseas regions, regardless of the political objectives that might motivate an enemy to move against a U.S. ally. It has a stake in the prevention of turmoil, regardless of the victim's status as an ally or an ideological neutral. It has a stake in the tranquility of the world's trading areas, regardless of the likelihood (or unlikelihood) that an aggressive act would lead, domino fashion, to more direct threats against the United States. What should unite all Free World peoples in a commitment to collective security, then, is not just ideological alignment. Nor is what makes it necessary for the United States to resist aggression abroad simply a persistent identity of the allies' security interests. Absent either the political or the traditional strategic rationale for a U.S. peacekeeping presence abroad, economic interdependence would establish a justification for local deterrence throughout the area of the U.S. overseas outreach. This justification originates in the requisites of any functioning economy.

The Requisites of an Interdependent Economy

A functioning economic system requires, in addition to a network of financial and industrial institutions, a supporting structure of peacekeeping institutions. Thus, the liberal trading zone of the 1950s and 1960s required low tariffs, high liquidity, easy convertability of currencies, and efficient institutions of global financial intermediation. It also required a general expectation of security and stability. Muggers and pirates can break down any trading system, from the neighborhood shopping center to the world market.

To suggest that the active aim of U.S. policy in the 1980s should be the restoration of the liberal vision, therefore, is to suggest redoubled emphasis on opening the doors to international trade and on keeping the peace throughout the zones of global commerce.

Opening the Doors

Much of the current disarray within the circle of Free World trading partners results from pressure by former U.S. clients to set independent—and increasingly protectionistic—international economic policies. What is more, they prefer to do so without sharing proportionate responsibilities for providing the fabric of common security on which the stability of the trading area depends.

To reverse the protectionistic trends of the 1980s will require that statesmen hold a spacious vision of their long-term national interests. It will require, too, some domestic political courage: Neither the AFL-CIO, nor the Japanese Ministry of Trade and Industry, nor French vintners hurting from Italian competition in ordinary wines need be expected to lead their respective nations' charges back toward universal free trade. Statesmen will have to act, if they act at all, against the entrenched interests of some of their most powerful bureaucracies and constituencies.

U.S. statesmen will have an especially difficult burden to bear. Restoration of the liberal vision will require a willingness on their part to use some of the clout that the United States has been disinclined to employ on the international stage since the loss in Vietnam.

Time was when a powerful, self-confident United States could dictate the conditions of development and trade within the Bretton Woods and GATT systems. The post-World War II U.S. hegemony depended on a combination of financial strength, intellectual ascendancy, and military strength. It depended in part on the nation's ability to play banker throughout the Free World: the United States had half of all the liquid reserves on the planet and accounted for half of the world's industrial product.[5] U.S. influence around the globe derived in part from the intellectual confidence that U.S. planners had in the schemes for interdependent economic growth that came from think tanks and universities.[6] However, the United States's ability to organize the liberal international economy also depended on its willingness to insist on a linkage between U.S. peacekeeping and the economic policies that were followed by the beneficiaries of that peacekeeping.

Alas, in the 1980s collective security has become unlinked from free trade. As it now stands, the United States bears a heavy extra-territorial security burden, but apparently not enough of a burden to guarantee an open international economy.

This anomaly reflects a view that has been propounded by some of the so-called regime theorists.[7] With the record of the Kissinger foreign policy of the 1970s before them, these theorists argue that international transactions tend to sort themselves into a military regime, a monetary regime, a tariff and trade regime, and so forth. The foreign policy of detente required linkage of the different regimes. Kissinger rightly thought that the Soviet Union wanted U.S. grain and an arms agreement; he wrongly thought that the United States could link grain sales and arms talks to Soviet good behavior in the Third World.[8]

The United States proved unable to translate its economic power into political leverage when trying to influence the Soviet Union's policies toward Angola and in the Horn of Africa.[9] Perhaps unduly influenced by the failure of linkage under Kissinger, the regime theorists argue that transactions within each issue area occur pretty much independently of transactions in other regimes. Allegedly, one country's military power can be used as leverage on another nation's tariff and trade policies only with difficulty—if at all.

If the regime theorists are right, then a universal free-trade zone can be purchased only by deals negotiated within the tariff and trade regime, that is, only by reciprocal free-trade agreements: You open up to our mousetraps, we will lower barriers to your widgets, or revalue our currency, or whatever. This is a caution of despair, however. If statesmen heed it, we all should strap in now for the final crash of the postwar liberal trading system. Although the economic principle of comparative advantage shows that free exchange promotes the long-run welfare of both trading partners, immediate political pressures by organized lobbies tend to win out over long-run economic considerations. Unemployed auto and steel workers have a better grip on the levers of U.S. and German policy than do the theorists of economic welfare (substitute agricultural workers in the French and Japanese cases, and textile workers in the British).

Thus, to attempt a reopening of the international economy using only the tools of economic diplomacy is to attempt the impossible. Bargaining on trade and monetary policies may take the Free World part way to an open international economy. However, more than strictly economic deals will be needed to complete the liberalization of the economic regime. An extra fillip will be necessary to take the Free World the rest of the way back to a liberal trading zone.

That fillip might take the form of a conditional U.S. provision of more manifest overseas peacekeeping services, especially in Asia. The condition of the provision should be the adoption of more liberal trade policies by the beneficiaries of those services. It is worth stressing that the Europeans, whose interdependence with the Asian trading countries is not in question, belong at the head of that list of potential beneficiaries. In other words, the United States should demand that its trading partners do more to open the doors of international commerce, if in exchange it does more to keep the peace within an expanding international trading area.

Keeping the Peace

For the better part of three decades after World War II, while U.S.-sponsored institutions such as the Bretton Woods monetary regime and GATT facilitated an increasing volume of international economic transactions, U.S. military forces policed the avenues of world commerce. During the era of nuclear superiority, the Strategic Air Command helped to do in the midtwentieth century what the Royal Navy had done in the nineteenth. Long-haul mercantile networks and long-term capital formation presuppose political-military stability, a requirement that was well understood by Great Britain, and especially by its engineers of global free trade who maintained the far-flung imperial basing system: Alexandria, Kingston, Gibraltar, Cape of Good Hope, Bombay, Singapore, Hong Kong.[10]

Today, not only the postwar monetary and industrial consensus shows signs of coming undone, but the peacekeeping apparatus also has fallen into disrepair. The causes of economic disarray trace, at least in part, to the worsening disrepair in the regime of international security.

It must be emphasized that it is not only protectionism that threatens a liberal international economy today. The physical peace of the U.S. overseas markets also has become uncertain. Since the early 1970s, the Soviet Union, Iran and Iraq, Libya, Vietnam—and, arguably, the Peoples' Republic of China, Israel, the Palestine Liberation Organization, North Korea, India and Pakistan, and Syria—have threatened law and order at one or more points around the Eurasian rim land. That is quite a record of hoodlum activity.

With prowlers in the neighborhood, men of commerce and property look to the adequacy of the local constabulary. However, a policeman's duties can be performed only if the policeman's presence is assured where the trouble may break out. The presence that is needed is not the virtual presence of force emanated over thousands of miles in a distant Rapid Deployment Force or in a nuclear threat of doubtful credibility (as in strategic coupling). What is needed is the actual presence of crack troops and fast ships in the neighborhood. These forces would have to be on call, as domestic police forces are on call, for quick action to contain local disorders. They would have to be visible, as domestic peacekeeping units are kept visible, to emanate power.[11] Such forces would have what Dulles used to call "local defense" as their main mission.[12] By presenting a credible ability to suppress threats to the peace of the neighborhood, they would fill the mission of local deterrence.

It is ironic that, during a period in which the growth of interdependence increased the need for an effective overseas local deterrent, the United States's commitment of forces to perform this mission has actually decreased—and most dramatically in the Western Pacific, where U.S. economic interests increasingly lie. Under the 1969 Nixon Doctrine, the United States would send aid but not troops in future Vietnam-type situations. The U.S. withdrawal from Indochina raised doubts about the United States's staying power when the going got tough and conceded an aggressive Vietnamese client (plus a big new naval base at Cam Ranh Bay) to the Soviet Union. President Carter's shilly-shallying on U.S. troop levels in South Korea created the worst of two worlds: the United States was left with the cost of maintaining continued deployments, but all the Pacific allies were left with uncertainty as to the reliability of a U.S. presence. Even in Europe, fears of "mansfieldism"—that is, of a U.S. ground troop withdrawal under the terms of the 1971 Mansfield Amendment—calls the exact nature of the United States's commitment into question.[13]

The Move to Relink

The exact nature of the U.S. overseas commitment cannot be fully set forth in advance of a long process of negotiation with the allies. The direction of change, however, can be predicted. In view of the failed record of nuclear threats as a deterrent to neighborhood crime, overseas security should take less the form of a strategic pledge and more the form of a visible peacekeeping presence. In view of U.S. geoeconomic interests around the world, the U.S. posture should be less in the nature of a community commitment to NATO Europe and Japan and more in the nature of a constabulary watch over the lines of economic interdependency. Finally, the implicit bargain with U.S. trading partners that would signal a move toward relinking probably also would call for the United States to bear relatively more—not less—of the overseas security burden.

In the 1980s, the United States cannot expect—or be expected—to reshoulder the full hegemonic burden of the 1950s. It cannot simultaneously play banker to the world, prime the pumps of economic growth, and provide the security umbrella of an almost universal pax americana. The United States should, however, perceive the continuing relationship between the provision of extraterritorial security and the attainment of foreign policy objectives on which its domestic prosperity depends. The aim must be to renew the linkage between strategy and economic policy that was lost in the 1970s. Linkage can still be made to work among allies, even if it failed as an instrument of detente between the superpowers.

To start the process of relinking, the United States must decide what kinds of military forces would best promote the objective of stabilizing a growing free-trade zone and then station them where they can do the job.

A Watch on the Asian Main

It is around the Asian Main that U.S. economic interests loom with increasing importance. Indeed, the Asian littoral encompasses the area in which a U.S. military presence can contribute most directly to the stability of the United States's—and, indeed, its European allies'—economic outreach.

Force planning for the Asian theater needs to be carried out with an eye toward a range of contingencies, including the contingency of a sudden frontal attack (say, across the 38th parallel in Korea). As the Soviet Union's Afghan invasion demonstrated, and as those forty-four Red Army divisions on the Chinese border continue to serve as a reminder, the Soviet Union can launch frontal attacks in areas where the United States has no formal treaty commitments, but whose security status can affect the Asian and even the world balance of power. However, as the Soviet Union also showed in Korea and Vietnam, the Asian rim land offers opportunities for the Kremlin leaders to play the game of competitive coexistence indirectly, by manipulating clients and proxies. The U.S. strategic focus should be on those contingencies that political restlessness in Asia makes most likely: contingencies in which the mechanisms of stabilization fail with or without conscious Soviet abetment, resulting in severe commercial disruptions (remember the gas lines of 1974 and 1980?) or local wars.

An Orchestration of Emphases

Diplomatically, the United States cannot present its trading partners with ultimatums. Nor can it write a single set of objectives for the outcome of future Economic Summits and GATT negotiations. Instead, the United States must try to set a diplomatic course toward free trade as a general goal. Then it must arrange a whole set of incentives that are geared toward the desired end. Finally, the United States must trust in a sustained process of give-and-take to move all the trading partners gradually closer to their goals.

The same holds true for force planning. Militarily and economically, the United States cannot expect to mount the overwhelmingly preponderant array of ground, sea, and air forces that President Reagan's defense advisers tried to sell to Congress. Nor, at the opposite extreme, can it build up one component of the overseas presence to the exclusion of the other elements that are needed in a balanced military force: No one service represents a total solution. However, a balanced military force can still be a force with a "bulge." It can be a force with a distinctive prominence to recognize the special needs of a particular mission. The mission to be emphasized around the Asian Main is not the safeguarding of ideological purity or political solidarity within a quondam anticommunist bloc, but the safeguarding of the commercial base from international hoodlumism. That mission calls for a distinctive pattern of emphasis (a naval emphasis) in U.S. Asian rim-land forces, just as the mission of frontal deterrence calls for a special force structure (a nuclear artillery force) on NATO's central front.

Two adjustments—apart from a naval build up of reasonable proportions—seem needed if the United States is to mount a successful watch on the Asian Main: a change in the orientation of U.S. ranger-type units (that is, the Rapid Deployment Joint Task Force, RDJTF), and a change in the U.S. basing posture around the rim land.

Ranger-Type Units for Air-Land Missions

Given a need to demonstrate the seriousness of the U.S. commitment in Asia, one's eyes must glaze over when reading official Pentagon documents that emphasize that the vaunted U.S. firefighting force has no units totally or permanently assigned to it.[14] Instead, the Rapid Deployment Task Force is an organizational blueprint for a fighting capability to be assembled, block by block, on the eve of deployment. Most of the RDJTF's divisions—one, a Marine Amphibious Force; another, an Army airborne division—and its twelve tactical air squadrons are simultaneously committed to the NATO conventional defense mission.[15] Even if one assumes that these units could contain a war in the Middle East, one can hardly make the further assumption that they would be able, while invested in battle somewhere near the Persian

Gulf, simultaneously to help deter the frontal push against Europe to which a U.S. success (let alone a U.S. failure) in the Middle East conceivably might lead.

Furthermore, given a need to reestablish a U.S. presence in Asia, one must doubt either the strategic soundness or the ingenuousness of official pronouncements to the effect that rearward-deployed units of the RDJTF could be moved with sufficient speed to a trouble spot abroad. Only the Marine Amphibious Force and the one assigned airborne division could deploy to Southwest Asia rapidly without the benefit of a friendly host-country's support in the form of land basing and secure logistics. RDJTF staff members themselves admit that— even with uncontested access to needed port facilities and overland lines of communication—more than a month would be needed to position heavy artillery or armored divisions.[16] Because the latter divisions would come from the NATO-committed contingents, the European flank would be exposed long before the needed thirty to forty days were up. These estimates tend to confirm the desirability of deemphasizing the conventional defense of NATO Europe, even as the United States profits from the resulting reduction in its trans-Atlantic military burden by diverting some resources to the local deterrent mission in Asia.

(Incidentally, a diversion of resources from frontal deterrence in Europe to local deterrence in Asia would not exactly equate to a full geographic redeployment of U.S. forces. Some RDJTF units could be fully committed to defend the Asian theater—and, more particularly, to defend the Persian Gulf oil on which the trilateral partners are so much more dependent than is the United States itself—but be left in Europe, where they would still be three-thousand miles closer to their designated operating area than if they were based in the continental United States).

For the countering of local probes, crack units such as the Marine Amphibious Force obviously could operate more effectively from positions in the theater than from rearward home bases. For more threatening contingencies, such as the sometimes-discussed Soviet frontal move against Iran, the United States would need artillery—preferably nuclear artillery, for all the reasons that apply to the frontal scenario in NATO Europe—capable of being used to maximum effect early in the course of the conflict.

An early first-use strategy in Asia would not necessarily entail the posting of large conscript armies to distant posts—doubtless a political impossibility in any case. For the enemy to know that the United States would be able to fight a frontal war in Asia successfully, however, the nation would need to have forces that could be committed there without dangerously weakening the U.S. deterrent posture in Europe. In addition, secure access to the overland facilities needed to back up a frontal war-waging posture in Asia would have to have been negotiated already. Those overland facilities, which of course would not need full garrisoning except in time of crisis, could be viewed as extensions of the seaward and coastal facilities around the Asian Main for which the United States also must negotiate. Frontal warfare in Asia, however, whether conventional or nuclear, should be seen as much less likely than contingencies involving local disturbances or sea-land disruptions. Frontal warfare should be eliminated altogether from the U.S. Asian military planning agenda until the RDJTF that would have to fight it has been restructured and until U.S. negotiations for bases and depots have ensured the preconditions for success.

A String of Bases and Depots

It will be necessary, then, in order to support the ranger-type forces that can best meet likely air-land requirements around the Asian Main, to negotiate for access to a string of overseas depots and outposts. The acquisition of staging and berthing facilities around the Asian Main would permit the United States to reestablish a potent presence throughout the old arc of military containment, albeit not a presence based on a 1950s-type fabric of integrated alliances. Overseas bases and depots should girdle the entire rim land, to signify that U.S. interests extend as equally to the Islamic crescent, the Indian subcontinent, and the economically dynamic Far East as they do to the Atlantic partners.

This image of a ring around the rim land governed the post-World War II quest for a globe-girdling string of airbases that, President Roosevelt's advisers emphasized, could serve both military and commercial purposes.[17] The ring of bases that the nation eventually developed from Turkey to Korea thence became key military and diplomatic buttresses of Dulles's foreign policy. According to that policy, militarily, the United States would rely on its strategic air forces, deployed in the encircling posture around the Soviet Union, to embody the threat of massive retaliation. Diplomatically, it would press for demonstrations of solidarity among all Free World nations. Under the rubric of global containment, the United States would cultivate an arc of integrated alliances (CENTRO-ANZUS-SEATO-Treaty of Friendship with Japan) to ensure stability around the Asian rim land.

Walter Lippmann, however, foretold that containment would commit the Untied States to a strength-sapping process of interference in the politics of corrupt and feeble client regimes all around the Asian Main—a process that, indeed, eventually led to the debacle of Vietnam.[18] However approvingly or invidiously one might characterize the existing regimes from the Middle East around to South Korea, few of these regimes today have unproblematical relations with the United States. Given the turmoil of the Middle East, given the pride that the Indians take in their posture of nonalignment, and given the resistance throughout East Asia to any appearance of client status, one sees little reason to think that the United States could, even if it should, return to the pattern of alliances that the early practitioners of containment stretched from the Middle East to Japan.

Instead, as both the military and the diplomatic buttresses of the 1950s have lost relevance given the conditions of the 1980s, the United States should return to the underlying structure—to that ring around the rim land—while reorienting the ring's military and diplomatic significance. In place of a strategic air-base system to support massive retaliation, the United States needs a network of naval depots and ports that also could serve as staging points for forward-deployed ranger-type peacekeeping forces. Instead of trying, as the early practitioners of containment tried, to color broad areas of the world map blue so as to signify formal Western alignment, the United States now needs a series of points on the map so configured as to display renewed U.S. resolve, but also so arrayed as to minimize U.S. involvement in the domestic politics or the regional tensions of Asia. Again: the United States's primarily economic interests call for a pattern designed to promote stability in an intercontinental trading zone, rather than a bloc based on a common political ideology.

A program to secure strategic strongholds and staging bases, instead of one to revitalize a moribund system of integrated alliances, has a precedent in the 1939 lend-lease agreements. However, major facilities at, say, the island of Diego Garcia in the Indian Ocean, instead of at the eastern gateways to the Caribbean, would define the object of U.S. interest in the 1980s. U.S. base rights in Japan (including Okinawa) and the Philippines witness to a structure of outposts that is already partly in place. Doubts about the Greek commitment to NATO, about the possibility of a permanent strategic consensus with Israel, about the adequacy of the logistical infrastructure in the area of the Horn of Africa and the Arabian Sea, and about the United States's ability to secure the sea lines of communication around Southeast Asia, however, indicate that a really firm structure of forward bases and depots yet needs to be completed.

Better forward naval and air-land staging bases are most urgently required in the Indian Ocean—even more so, probably, than in the stretch from the Malacca Strait up to Japan. U.S. interests in the Indian Ocean imply a need for facilities at points such as Masirah Island off the coast of Oman, in the tiny country of Bahrain overlooking the Persian Gulf, at Diego Garcia in the British Chagos Archipelago, and possibly in Australia—not the mere skeleton facilities for which provision has already been made, but well-developed bases on the pattern of those that serve U.S. forces in the Philippines, Japan, and Korea.

(Mention of Australia recalls Churchill's idea of a league of English-speaking peoples. To the extent that cultural images have continuing validity—as they clearly do—they might evoke a U.S.-Australian-British association more powerfully than they do a revivified Atlantic Community. Such an association would support intensive development of the naval base at Inverness in Scotland for defense against the Soviet northern fleet, and a U.S.-Australian agreement for intensive use of the port at Darwin—from a geostrategic standpoint, potentially the new Singapore in a network of bases around the southern seas.)

Naval Structure and Strategy

As has been suggested already, the emphasis in complementing the network of bases should be on a powerful fleet—not on a less-than-credible strategic nuclear threat or on a less-than-ready RDJTF stationed in the continental United States. A powerful fleet probably remains the best way to show the flag in quarters of the globe that are of vital interest to an island-nation with critical overseas markets and resource dependencies.

A fleet that is designed primarily to emanate power needs to assert a continuing presence. Therefore, a constabulary navy operating from a series of bases around the Asian Main should be able to cover missions in the Western Pacific without sacrificing the capability to display force in the Indian Ocean, or vice versa. In other words, the mission of stabilizing the United States's international economic outreach underlines the need for a large navy, although the final figure in President Reagan's naval objective force—600 to 650 ships—may be extravagant. Moreover, the mix of ships envisioned in President Reagan's navy may be poorly suited to the mission of local deterrence of international hoodlum activity around the rim land.[19]

Broadly speaking, the competitors for dominance within the U.S. navy are the proponents of submarines, of aircraft carriers, and of modern gunboats.

As instruments of stealth, submarines' primary operational uses lie in tactics that do not display their punch until after they have been used. In the right circumstances, a submarine can be a wondrously capable killer of surface ships and can be adapted to the ASW mission as well. However, it cannot easily deploy modulated force—cannot put the proverbial shot across an opponent's bow without tilting the odds to its own disadvantages, because it cannot reveal its presence without compromising its survivability.[20] The mission of visibly displaying force with the hope of deterring military action is not high on the list of jobs for which subsurface vessels are well suited.

As was noted in chapter 3, the U.S. navy has for years been organized around carriers and their associated battle groups. The Reagan planners' desire to add two Nimitz-class flattops, with the full complement of battle-group supporting vessels, would intensify the traditional bias. As centerpieces of elaborate naval battle groups, however, these large carriers may lack the economy and flexibility that is needed for discriminating assignment over a range of possible missions. Moreover, big carriers would present attractive targets for relatively cheap smart weapons. Even when he knows his flagship to be protected by the costly escort vessels of the full battle group, a carrier admiral must awaken periodically with the awful vision of what that French-made Exocet missile did to H.M.S. Sheffield during the Falklands War. Finally, carrier battle groups probably are less cost effective than are alternative ship systems (including submarine packs) for convoy protection and ASW.

However, the Reagan defense planners apparently had missions other than sea-lane keeping and antisubmarine warfare in mind when they moved to accelerate the program for a carrier-centered navy that President Carter had already laid down. The Reagan planners had in mind a new grand strategy to replace the strategy of vertical escalation, a strategy that would require multiple carrier groups. It is worth a brief digression to consider the proposed new doctrine, called space-time escalation, because its adoption or rejection will decisively influence the composition of the navy with which the United States enters the twenty-first century.[21]

Space-Time Escalation

Space-time escalation includes the notions of horizontal escalation (escalation in space by hitting the enemy with conventional forces wherever U.S. planners feel most sure of scoring a military victory, rather than meeting the enemy's forces where they have already claimed the initiative) and protracted conflict (escalation in time by drawing the Soviet

Union into a conventional war of attrition, in which U.S. industrial and logistical superiority eventually will prove to be decisive).

A large navy operating on all of the world's major oceans would, of course, provide the vehicle for the single or multiple ripostes that the United States would take in response to a Soviet move. In theory, carrier-centered battle groups would let the United States take the war to the enemy by striking with overwhelming conventional force at his home land—using U.S. surface-naval superiority instead of the now-vanished U.S. nuclear superiority to countervail against the numerical superiority of the Soviet ground forces. In yet another variant of the naval strategy of horizontal escalation, a move by the Red Army into Persian Gulf oil fields, for example, could call forth a direct U.S. countermove in the form of RDJTF deployment, plus naval air attacks against Soviet submarine pens serving the Pacific, a blockade of the approaches to and from Murmansk by way of the Norwegian Sea, a show of force as U.S. battle groups steam southward for World War II-type naval action against the Soviet fleet in the Indian Ocean, and interdiction of Soviet trade with client states (for example, Cuba). The scenario might end up with the United States's actual bombardment and invasion of such an interdicted Soviet client. Or, as Secretary of Defense Weinberger once suggested, U.S. troops might recover Vietnam or move in Korea for a final settlement of scores with Pyongyang in order to counter a Soviet-engineered attack where U.S. decision makers felt unsure of Western strength—such as in Berlin, the North German Plain, Turkey, or elsewhere in the Middle East.[22]

Space-time escalation concedes the military initiative to the enemy by inviting the Soviet Union to pursue its interests seriatim as opportunities present themselves. It also concedes local victories to the enemy, so long as he can rig the odds to his own advantage at the start of a war by probing only where the United States would have trouble meeting force with proportionate force. The Soviet Union inevitably will have a huge advantage in any conventional ground war around the rim land unless U.S. outlays for naval forces to offset the Soviet geostrategic edge stretch the very limits of U.S. national economic capacities.[23]

Given the Soviet Union's geostrategic advantages, the adoption of space-time escalation also could invite Soviet decision makers to contrive a series of trades based on calculated, limited moves: for example, the Soviet Union takes Berlin, knowing that the United States is likely to take, say, Cuba in exchange. The United States would thereby tidy up its Caribbean backyard, and, into the bargain, the Soviet Union would save a $3 billion annual levy on its economy and gain a major propaganda victory in Latin America. Or again: the Soviet Union probes in Iran, Pakistan, or even (via Afghanistan or Iran) into the Persian Gulf oilfields. The United States counters by taking . . . what? North Korea? Angola? Vietnam?

A series of such trades gradually would redraw the lines of global influence to the detriment of the United States. The Soviet Union could pick off the high-value targets on its rim-land agenda in salami-slice wars, leaving the United States to take face-saving victories in return—victories in locales of lesser importance to both contestants. For this reason, space-time escalation looks to a course of evolution in the global order that runs directly counter to a basic post-World War II U.S. aim. It looks, not to the imagery of a pluralistic globe, nor to an era in which economic development and commercial exchange—rather than ideological antagonism—dominates statecraft, but instead to Stalin's imagery of a globe divided into mutually exclusive spheres of influence along lines of relative geostrategic strength—precisely the imagery that the United States tried to reject at Yalta and Postdam and certainly an imagery that offers little hope for a revitalized liberal world order.[24] As such, space-time escalation represents a dangerous detour from the general direction of U.S. post war foreign policy.

Given that a revitalized liberal world order will require a revitalized liberal economy, the appropriate strategic course lies not in an approach (such as space-time escalation) that invites global division nor in an imagery (such as the imagery associated with the Atlantic Community) that diverts attention from the economically dynamic sectors of a future global trading system. Rather, the appropriate course lies in the direction of forces and strategies that would promote stability within the economically critical zone by deterring the kinds of threats—those threats of international hoodlumism, whether Soviet-inspired or not—that present the main danger.

A Gunboat Navy

A surface fleet consisting mainly of cruisers, frigates, and destroyers—a gunboat navy—may be the best instrument yet devised for emanating power. Combine such a fleet with sophisticated antisubmarine capabilities, add a fast sea-lift capacity to serve those forward staging bases that the United States needs around the Asian Main and, if need be, reinforce them in the event of war, and the primary constabulary as well as probable war-waging requirements in the Indian Ocean and Western Pacific would be met pretty well. Critical components of the resulting force structure, compared with elements envisioned by planners of the Reagan build up, are summarized in table 6–1.

Table 6–1
Critical Components of U.S. Posture in Asia under Alternative Strategies

	Current Force Level	Planned: Late 1980s- Early 1990s	Needed for Rim-Land Strategy
Aircraft carriers	13	15	14
Gunboats	179	215	215
Total battle groups	13	15	14
Of which dedicated to North Atlantic	6	6	4
Of which dedicated to Asian Main			
West of Malacca Strait	2	3	4
North of Malacca Strait	5	6	6
Total attack subs	96	107	107
Of which dedicated to North Atlantic	41	41	37
Of which dedicated to Asian Main			
West of Malacca Strait	–	10	35
North of Malacca Strait	35	35	35
Assault and lift			
Amphibious and landing ships	66	76	76
Airlift—intercontinental	326	413	413
Sealift—fast and reserve	51	72	72
Army-Marine RDJTF Divisions[a]			
Airborne, cavalry, infantry—active	2-⅓	3-⅓	2-½
Armored and mechanized	1-⅓	1-⅓	1
Conventional and nuclear artillery	–	–	1
Marine Amphibious Force	1	1	2
Total active RDJTF divisions	5-⅔	6-⅔	6-½
Prepositioned division sets			
West of Malacca Strait	1	1-⅔	3
Base, Depot host countries			
West of Malacca Strait			
Major permanent base areas	–	1	2
Limited access or utility	1	2	3
Skeleton or stopover	6	4	6
North of Malacca Strait			
Major permanent base areas	3	3	3
Limited access or utility	2	2	2
Skeleton or stopover	6	6	6

Source: Author's estimates adapted from *U.S. Military Posture for FY 1982* (Washington, D.C.: U.S. Government Printing Office, 1981), 44-45, 71; Caspar Weinberger, *Annual Report to Congress for FY 1983* (Washington, D.C.: U.S. Department of Defense, 1982), III-36, 93, 97-99; Jeffrey Record, "The Rapid Deployment Force: Problems, Constraints, and Needs," *Annals* 109 (September 1981):117-118; *World Military and Social Expenditures, 1982* (Leesburg, Va.: World Priorities Publications, 1982), 8.
[a]RDJTF: Rapid Deployment Joint Task Force.

A decision to emphasize a gunboat navy would not, however, finally settle the issue of carrier procurement. The $7 billion decision on construction of the next two Nimitz-class carriers represents a critical point of contact between naval force planning to emanate U.S. power in the waters around the rim land and planning for the role of U.S. theater nuclear forces in possible land wars on the Eurasian continent.

The U.S. first-use threat applies primarily to the mission of frontal deterrence in Europe, but it also would implicitly reserve the nuclear option for use in appropriate tactical circumstances in Asia—say, to stop a Red Army frontal move against the Persian Gulf or a North Korean attack across the 38th parallel. Should the United States serve up natural and obvious targets for an enemy to hit with nuclear weapons? Carriers would present prime targets for Soviet nuclear retaliation, should they be put on station within reach of enemy land-based aircraft—as they would have to be, in order to serve as floating bases in support of U.S. tactical air strikes against enemy units. It is in the nature of a carrier group at sea to present a counterforce target capable of being hit with minimum collateral destruction. It is, in a sense, then, in the nature of a large aircraft carrier to invite a nuclear attack in a way that no land-based unit—not even a massed armored formation— does.

On the other hand, a rim-land strategy calls for a string of bases all around the Asian Main, whether in the form of unsinkable carriers (such as the islands of Masirah, Diego Garcia, and Guam would represent) or in the form of movable islands (such as the proposed new supercarriers would represent). Within broad limits, the two types of bases can be substituted for each other. Whereas the United States must negotiate for island basing rights and foreign naval berths, the decision to build a new carrier lies within U.S. control—provided, of course, that the nation is willing to pony up the $3.5 billion going price for each flattop (exclusive of aircraft), plus the extra $10 to $15 billion that is needed to round out a supporting escort group.

Optimally, the United States would continue supercarrier procurement on a stretched-out basis, putting carrier construction into a kind of slow motion. If negotiations for a satisfactory ring of ports and depots around the rim land were to fall short of desired results, a rim-land strategy still could be premised on the availability of carriers for service in the Indian and Pacific Oceans rather than on the series of basing facilities. On the other hand, should negotiations produce satisfactory results, a stretched-out carrier construction program could be stopped at acceptable cost.

A Constabulary Presence, A Rim-Land Strategy

The mission of local deterrence, like that of frontal deterrence, presents different kinds of challenges in the European and the Asian contexts.

In the former, the looming presence of Warsaw Pact armored forces in Eastern Europe, combined with the delicacy of the European equipoise, heightens the danger that a local incident or a globally deteriorating political situation could trigger the long-feared frontal attack against NATO. Deterrence of that attack becomes the appropriate aim of U.S. strategy. Thus, in Europe, local deterrence holds a position subordinate to the frontal deterrent mission. Correspondingly, the conventional force posture in Europe, though in need of improvement, presents a secondary line of defense, while a posture of nuclear resistance carries the main message of U.S. resolve.

The orders of priority are reversed around the Asian Main: local deterrence and a suitable conventional posture are primary; frontal deterrence and nuclear strategies figure less importantly. Mischief-making at multiple points around the Asian littoral, not massive frontal assaults by the Soviet Union, pose the real threat. Today's enemies are the international equivalents of local toughs who unsettle the peace of the neighborhood, whether acting under Soviet provocation or under motivations that have no relation to the East-West competition. Indeed, from the standpoint of the U.S. economic interest in promoting a stable trading zone, the consequential factor in the Asian equilibrium is not ideological competition but the danger of turmoil, irrespective of the troublemaker's motives. The deterrence of such outbreaks—local deterrence—defines the main mission of U.S. conventional forces in the Asian theaters.

The mission of local deterrence around the Asian Main points toward a force structure specially tailored to promote stability within the trading area whose development is interdependent with the United States's—a force structure that displays U.S. commitment by establishing a powerful countervailing presence, but without unduly involving the United States in other peoples' ideological or political choices. These ostensibly inconsistent goals—promoting economic interdependence while respecting political independence; establishing a national presence while eschewing unnecessary involvements—can best be reconciled in an off-shore posture whereby the physical deployment of forces becomes a metaphor for U.S. detachment from the internal concerns of those with whom the United States wants to deal.

Forward-based air-land units—in effect, a redesigned RDJTF stationed, for the most part, overseas—could meet ground-war missions below some critical threshold. Classically, such missions have defined the situations for calling in the marines or relying on ranger-type forces. It is not coincidental that marine and ranger forces have always been thought of as crack units, to be carried with the fleet or else to be forward deployed with the mission of ranging from base to base in distant frontier areas. The point is: The air-land forces that should be mounted to deal with credible ground-war contingencies around the Asian rim land can be fit readily into a pattern that emphasizes the naval component of a U.S. presence abroad and that looks to a series of secure base points rather than to an area of tightly aligned countries.

The transition from a strategy conceived in the imagery of an integrated alliance system—what the former Pentagon official Robert Komer approvingly called a coalition defense—to one designed on the template of a far-flung network of bases would be consistent with the imagery of a U.S. island-nation in a multipolar world.[25] This imagery in no way implies a rejection of alliances. However, it does imply a recognition of the loosening that has already occurred within the old containment structure.

To recognize the multipolar nature of the contemporary world order also is to recognize that a new equilibrium in relations between a relatively weaker but still formidably powerful United States and less tractable but still Western-oriented allies must be found. The needed new equilibrium could result from a bargain in which the United States bears not a total, but a disproportionate, Free World security burden. Instead of repaying in kind by appreciably increasing their defense outlays and integrating their forces with those of the United States, the allies' portion of the bargain could lie in more wholehearted participation in a liberal international economy. Value given, in the form of overseas security, should be linked to an expectation of value received, in the form of more open trade policies as the allies' quid pro quo. Surely there exists some level of increased U.S. defense outlays, particularly for overseas conventional forces, at which the reopening of a global trading area could make the package a good deal for U.S. taxpayers as well as for the allies.

The value that the allies would lose—as a result of a reduced U.S. strategic nuclear commitment—cannot be weighed against the value that they would gain if the United States quit nagging them to boost their defense contribution and just went ahead on its own to post a guard around the rim land. What weight a different commitment (constabulary presence instead of strategic threat) in a different configuration (a rim-land emphasis instead of a trilateral one) would have in negotiations toward a relinking of collective security to international trade cannot be predicted. However, it can be said that U.S. interests lie in the direction of patient movement toward a new foreign policy based on decoupling or relinking or—most likely—a bit of both.

7 Conclusion: Special Strategies

How does the United States get from here to there—to a posture that combines an effective global military capability with affordability? To one that strikes a prudent mean between decoupling and relinking—while recognizing that neither policy will win many hurrahs from U.S. clients abroad?

It should be made clear all around—to the allies, to the nonaligned, and, of course, to adversaries—that the United States means, over time, to

1. Decouple the strategic nuclear forces from the overseas theaters;
2. Redesign the strategic triad to meet the narrowly defined mission of primary deterrence;
3. Retain a battlefield nuclear option so as to stabilize the secondary deterrent in Europe following the withdrawal of the strategic nuclear pledge;
4. Eliminate general requirements for American military actions beyond the North-South fault line, except insofar as Third World unrest threatens the U.S. economic outreach around the Asian Main;
5. Secure the U.S. economic outreach by reestablishing a U.S. naval presence around the Asian portion of the rim land and, as a corollary
6. Negotiate for secure forward depots and bases on the Asian Main, with the aim of servicing a modernized gunboat navy and ranger-type forces stationed near likely local trouble spots;
7. Relink international economics to overseas security by pressing all the beneficiaries of a rim-land strategy to adopt more agreeable trade, monetary, and investment policies.

In order to advance this seven-step agenda, a new imagery will be needed in U.S. foreign policy.

Imagery and Policy

The familiar imagery of community hurts the United States in three ways: its distorts the citizens' view of the nation's true long-range in-

113

terests abroad; it gives meretricious support to a military posture of diminishing credibility; and it promotes a growing paralysis of strategic thought by fostering an imagery of holocaust.

The image of community—whether envisioned as an Atlantic Community or as a broader trilateral partnership—distracts the United States from its true economic interests as an island-nation. As an island people, U.S. citizens are increasingly interdependent with precisely those trading centers around the Asian Main that lie beyond the traditional boundaries of the U.S. protectorate in Europe and Northeast Asia.

Even within those boundaries—and notwithstanding the communitarian sentimentality that the United States's special relationships with Western Europe and Japan have encouraged—the pledge to hostage its own people for any value other than the nation's own security suffers from a bad case of diminishing credibility. The waning credibility of the U.S. pledge has undermined the United States's postwar posture of extended deterrence. At the same time, the nation's professed reliance on a potentially suicidal pledge has dulled the sense of urgency with which it should be moving to put something else in place so as to secure the frontal deterrent in Europe. The deftness with which the United States deemphasizes the extended strategic deterrent while upgrading the steadfastness of the forward frontal deterrent will determine, in large part, the future of U.S. relations with West Germany. Much of the argument presented in chapter 5 turns on the assumption that, in comparison with the continuing vexations of the German problem, the problem of achieving a semblance of sweet unity within the NATO alliance as a whole is of decidedly subordinate concern.

What is needed within the old Atlantic Community is not runaway mansfieldism, whereby the United States suddenly would yank its boys back home, leaving a politically and strategically destabilized Europe behind. Rather, what is needed is an agenda for sustained negotiations. The NATO partners' expectations must be put on a new basis—no more suicide pact; no more free rides. At the same time, U.S. allies have the right to suppose that actual changes in U.S. policies and deployments will come gradually. This concept of NATO diplomacy differs from the position of those who urge the United States to give Europe a take-it-or-leave-it ultimatum of immediate U.S. disengagement. However, it also differs from the concept behind those periodic NATO ministerial get togethers, whose main objective apparently is to put a good common face on the deepening disarray within the alliance. It is time to redeploy energies, from the process of cosmetizing the natural dissolution of an unnatural community to the process of negotiating a U.S.-German bargain.

Finally, the imagery of community, when given expression in the strategic nuclear pledge, leads to an imagery of holocaust. Under the one-for-all promise that expresses the communitarian ideal, any threat to the community may lead to war. Under the doctrine of strategic coupling, any war in Europe may lead to a superpower exchange—to armageddon.

As long as U.S. strategic doctrine continues to evoke the imagery of holocaust in this way, the pressures of self-deterrence scarcely can fail to bear more and more powerfully on U.S. decision makers. Self-deterrence, which further undermines the credibility of the strategic nuclear threat, has, in its natural course, led to calls for no first use and for a corrective upgrading of U.S. conventional forces, especially in NATO Europe. As a result of these calls, the pendulum of U.S. defense policy seems to be swinging from one general strategy to another.

The Trouble with General Strategies

Nuclear fears penetrate all strata of European and American society, and apparently have gained a constituency in the Soviet Union as well. Among U.S. defense thinkers, the sense of nuclear dread finds outlet in the move to reject the last vestige of the general strategy of massive retaliation—the vestige that flexible response retained by posing a continuing threat of strategic nuclear reprisals as a way of deterring Soviet frontal aggression. Unfortunately, however, the publicists of the new dispensation would replace the old general strategy with a close facsimile of a new general strategy.

Under the new strategy, the United States would respond with beefed-up conventional forces to frontal aggression as well as to local incidents, Soviet probes, and proxy wars. Unfortunately, too, the proponents of no first use prefer a course of action that might prove to be unaffordable even if the United States could count on its allies for financial help. And the conventional panacea probably would ruin the domestic economy if the United States should try unilaterally to upgrade the nonnuclear defense of the trilateral region. Thus, the proponents of no first use end up with no more credible—and much more expensive—a strategy than was the strategy of massive retaliation. As the figures in table 7–1 suggest, the conventional build up that probably would be needed to compensate for a no-first-use pledge would cost almost as much as would the critical components in the Reagan administration's program that already has proved impossible to push through Congress. Indeed, if no first use failed to yield an economic dividend in the form of cutbacks in critical strategic nuclear programs (MX, B-

Table 7–1
Probable Requirements to Meet Reagan Administration or No-First-Use Goals
(in billions of dollars)

	First Use Retained		No First Use	
	Probable Program	*Five-year Outlays*	*Probable Program*	*Five-year Outlays*
Strategic forces coupled to NATO				
Minuteman III		$ –		$ –
MX, 100	Deploy	16.5	Cut 25	12.38
Midgetman, 250	Deploy	8.0	Deploy	8.0
B-1, 100	Deploy	28.3	Cut 25	21.23
Stealth	IOC 1995	5.0	Slow up	3.5
Bomber Alert		–		–
Trident II SLBM	Deploy	5.9	Deploy	5.9
U.S. contribution, NATO upgrading				
Pershing II	Deploy	2.0	Cancel	–
Tomahawk-G	Deploy	1.5	Cancel	–
Neutron warheads		–		–
New tanks	Add 6,400	8.5	Add 8,400	10.0
Antitank, PGM	Upgrade	1.5	Upgrade	2.5
Army, Marine divisions				
Active	Add 1	4.5	Add 4	14.0
Reserve	Add 2	2.0	Add 2	2.0
Prepos div sets	Add 2	1.5	Add 4	3.0
Tactical air wings				
Active	Add 4	7.6	Add 5	9.6
Reserve	Add 2	2.5	Add 4	5.0
RDJTF and other, Asian emphasis[a]				
Nimitz carriers	Add 2	7.0	Add 1	3.5
Gunboats	Add 34	18.0	Add 20	12.0
Attack submarines	Add 11	5.0	Add 11	5.0
Amphibious and landing	Add 10	2.0	Add 10	2.0
Airlift, Sealift	Upgrade	7.2	Upgrade	7.2
Active airborne, infantry	Add 1 division	4.5	Add 1 division	4.5
Conventional and nuclear artillery		–		–
Rangers, MAFs	Upgrade	1.5	Upgrade	1.5
Prepos div sets	Add 1 set	0.5	Add 1 set	0.5
Base acquis and impr	D. Garcia	1.0	D. Garcia	1.0
Naval presence	Flt exer	1.75	Flt exer	1.75
		$143.75		$136.06

Source: Author's estimates adapted from William Kaufmann, *Defense in the 1980s* (Washington, D.C.: Brookings Institute, 1982), 23, 44, 46-49; Kaufmann, "The Defense Budget," in *Setting National Priorities: The Fiscal 1983 Budget,* ed. J. Pechman (Washington, D.C.: Brookings Institute, 1982), 67, 76, 82, 87, 91-92; Kaufmann, *The Fiscal 1984 Budget* (Washington, D.C.: Brookings Institute, 1983), 61, 73; and Earl Ravenal, "The Case for Withdrawal of Our Forces," *The New York Times Magazine,* 6 March 1983, 60.

[a]RDJTF: Rapid Deployment Joint Task Force.

1, Stealth), then it would cost significantly more than the generally nuclear-oriented Reagan program.

The dilemma of credibility versus affordability cannot be escaped by swinging from one general strategy to its opposite. A single, all-purpose formula for dealing with the three kinds of threats that the United States faces—an ultimate central threat, possible frontal threats (especially in Europe), and a set of local threats (especially in Asia)—cannot be written.

Nor, it seems, is the United States even likely to be able to frame appropriate special strategies until the threats that it faces have been revisualized using the imagery of an escalatory network.

Escalation and an Imagery of Limits

At every level of threat, the gravest danger derives from the possibility of incremental escalation or conflict expansion: local social or political turmoil erupting into local warfare; a local conflict triggering a series of limited wars or even a frontal attack; a frontal war so destabilizing in its impact on the global equilibrium of power that one side's leaders, seeing little to lose by further escalation, raise the stakes by launching a central strike.

Massive retaliation would have sought to limit a fire in Asia or Europe by dousing it with gasoline. Massive retaliation threatened escalation—not in a series of incremental jumps, but in a single swoop to punish an aggressor, irrespective of the locale or level of the provocation. Yet it is not clear that the strategic concepts of the 1960s and 1970s would do much to block the pathways of escalation, either. The advocates of those concepts went to the opposite extreme from massive retaliation. Ever since the advocates of flexible response successfully made their case against Dulles's strategy, U.S. force planning has been driven by the continuing quest for a full spectrum of military capabilities. If massive retaliation provided for a small force of strategic bombers capable only of large-scale responses, the reformers of the 1960s and 1970s sought a large-scale military capability with the ability to inflict graduated damage on an enemy. Possession of the continuum of force presumably would let the United States meet the enemy at any level of conflict.

However, the affordability of the continuum of force depends critically on the mix of systems that compose it. If there is no mix—or if there is no realistic balance between conventional and nuclear systems within the mix—then there is no way to fund a full spectrum. The prohibitive costliness of the general strategy of conventional defense derives from its proponents' desire to mount nonnuclear systems capable of operating at every point along the continuum from local to frontal conflict. As a corrective change in emphasis against the background of massive retaliation, full-spectrum force planning made considerable sense. However, when it is made into a general strategy for both local and frontal deterrence, it heads straight for the economic horn of the defense dilemma.

The figures in table 7–2 suggest that a suitable mix of conventional and nuclear systems, when set in the context of a revised strategic force structure—and even when further adjusted for a significant Asian-oriented naval build up—can produce substantial savings by comparison with both the Reagan planners' across-the-board build up and the conventional build up that no first use probably would require.

The limitations of full-spectrum force planning do not end with the red ink that it would cause to flow, however. There is, in addition to an economic limitation, a strategic flaw in the concept of a continuum of capabilities. It lies in the difficulty that the concept presents to the task of sending appropriate signals to the enemy: signals of resolve combined with intended restraint.

Resolve and Restraint

The challenges of resolve and restraint present different orders of difficulty at the different levels of conflict. The Soviet Union presumably does not question the United States's intention to retaliate in the event of a Soviet attack on the U.S. home land. However, almost everyone questions decision makers' ability to exercise nuclear restraint if there should ever be a superpower exchange. It is a challenge of formidable difficulty to design a strategic retaliatory force that would promote both sides' observation of restraints in the waging of a central nuclear war. The dyadic force structure suggested in chapter 4 represents one approach to the problem of strategic restraint.

At the other end of the spectrum, both superpowers have displayed restraint in the amount of force that they could or would bring to bear in conflicts that did not manifestly engage their vital interests. It is not the United States's willingness to exercise restraint that is in question around the Asian Main, but rather its resolve—precisely the opposite of the situation that exists at the strategic level.

Alas, at the frontal level, an ultimately insupportable doctrine of strategic coupling, combined with fears of the escalation proneness of a nuclear ground war—further compounded by skepticism about the affordability of a conventional build up—have cast doubt on both the

Table 7–2
Program Changes and Cost Savings Possible with Special Strategies
(in billions of dollars)

		Savings Compared With	
		Probable Program with First Use	*Conventional Build Up with No First Use*
Primary Deterrence **with Strategic Decoupling**			
Minuteman III	Retrofit single reentry vehicles	$ –	$ –
MX	Cancel	16.5	12.38
Midgetman	Cancel	8.0	8.0
B-1	Cancel	28.3	21.3
Stealth	Advance IOC to 1989	(15.0)	(16.5)
Bomber Alert	Increase from 30 to 50 percent	(4.0)	(4.0)
Trident II SLBM	Cancel	5.9	5.9
Frontal deterrence **with early first use**			
Pershing II	No deployment	1.0	(1.0)
Tomahawk-G	No deployment	0.75	(0.75)
Neutron warheads	Deploy for artillery	1.0	1.0
New tanks	Cut procurement by half	4.25	5.0
Antitank, PGM	Upgrade	(1.5)	(0.75)
Army, Marine divisions			
Active	Cut two from current level	13.5	21.0
Reserve	Hold current level	2.0	2.0
Prepos div sets	Cut one from current level	2.25	3.75
Tactical air wings			
Active	Cut one from current level	9.2	11.5
Reserve	Hold current level	2.5	5.0
Local deterrence **on the Asian Main**			
Nimitz Carriers	Stretch out construction	3.5	–
Gunboats	Add twenty to current level	6.0	–
Attack submarines	Convert eleven Polaris, Poseidon	1.5	1.5
Amphibious and landing	Add ten to current level	–	–
Airlift, sealift	Expand and upgrade	–	–
Active airborne, infantry	Cut one brigade	5.0	5.0
Conventional and nuclear artillery	Add one div equiv	(4.5)	(4.5)
Rangers, MAFs	Add one MAF	(5.0)	(5.0)
Prepos div sets	Add two sets	(0.5)	(0.5)
Base acq and impr	Accelerate, expand	(9.0)	(9.0)
Naval presence	Double time on station	(1.75)	(1.75)
Net five-year savings		$ 69.70	$ 59.58

Source: Author's estimates adapted from William Kaufmann, *Defense in the 1980s* (Washington, D.C.: Brookings Institute, 1982) 23, 44, 46-49; Kaufmann, "The Defense Budget," in *Setting National Priorities: The Fiscal 1983 Budget* ed. J. Pechman (Washington, D.C.: Brookings Institute, 1982), 67, 76, 82, 87, 91-92; and Kaufmann, *The Fiscal 1984 Budget* (Washington, D.C.: Brookings Institute, 1983), 61, 73.

United States's resolve and its ability to exercise restraint. If resolve equates to a pledge of strategic retaliation, then the nation already may have given up on the possibility of a restrained response to a Warsaw Pact frontal move. However, if the United States writes off any realistic hope of restraint, then the psychology of self-deterrence probably implies a want of resolve. The resulting doubts continue to propel the U.S. posture in NATO Europe toward the credibility horn of the defense dilemma.

The best way to signal resolve at all levels is to mount forces that will permit the United States to fight successfully at any level of conflict. Where U.S. statesmen have gone wrong is in supposing that a single type of weaponry could fill the strategic and the economic requirements of a full-spectrum force structure. Beneath a certain level of provocation, the incredibility of the nuclear deterrent belies a profession of resolve. Above a certain level, the unaffordability of the full-spectrum conventional posture does the same.

The best way to signal a determination to exercise restraint is by mounting forces that simply would deny the United States the capability, in the stress of war, of jumping easily from one level of conflict up the next higher level. It does little good to proclaim, as the proponents of flexible response incessantly proclaimed, that the United States will meet force with appropriate force if the enemy can attach no meaning to the term *appropriate*—that is, if the enemy can discern no boundaries or buffers that the United States will observe as limits in its own employment of force. The needed buffers would take various forms: distinctive force deployments—such as geographically differentiated basing of land-based and sea-based intercontinental missiles; explicit reliance on different types of weapons to fulfill the frontal and the local deterrent missions; special strategies to guide tactics and targeting at the different levels of conflict. The nation then would have not just a full spectrum but a differentiated spectrum. It could respond to enemy forces at any level with a special strategy (retaliatory or resistive) and with special forces (nuclear or conventional) tailored for action at that level and distinguishable from the strategies and forces that have been ticketed for other missions.

In several respects, the result would differ from what exists today. To begin with, the buffers against escalation would be more varied and discriminating than is the all-or-nothing firebreak between conventional and nuclear warfare. These buffers would mark out different segments on the spectrum of conflict and would imply the United States's adoption of a revised formula for deterrence:

1. The threat of a quick conventional response to a local probe, using forces that have a high likelihood of successful resistance in the locale without escalating to nuclear warfare; combined with
2. The threat of immediate resistance of enemy frontal movements, using battlefield nuclear weapons; and
3. The threat of graduated central retaliation for attacks on the U.S. homeland.

This segmented strategy, rather like a strategy of zonal defense in athletics, would assume the existence of a system of zones, regimes, or compartments. Forces suitable to the challenge presented in each zone in every area under U.S. protection would be fielded. Failure to hold a zone would not activate the next-higher level of response. The decision to escalate would lie with the enemy. (Strategic coupling and flexible response both put the burden of choice on the United States.)

To complete the dialectical relationship between restraint and resolve, the best way for the United States to convince the enemy not to escalate when faced with a loss at a given level of conflict is to display its own determination before the moment of danger arrives. That is, the best way for the country to impose restraint on the enemy while exercising it itself is to have already mounted the high-confidence capability to meet a stepped-up threat at the higher level of conflict.

U.S. forces for selective central nuclear retaliation, for frontal resistance, and for conventional responses to local breaches of the peace that touch U.S. economic interests around the rim land would be distributed in a geographic sense: the strategic dyad described in chapter 4, the battlefield nuclear forces of chapter 5, and chapter 6's forward-based conventional units would have broadly distinguishable geographic foci, corresponding respectively to the security of the U.S. home land from attack (primary deterrence), the steadfastness of the forward line in Europe (frontal deterrence), and the stability of the economic outreach throughout the trading centers of the Asian Main (local deterrence). Although lead-service assignments can never be truly exclusive, primary planning and targeting responsibilities at the strategic level appropriately would go to the Air Force—which probably also would have operational control of the submarine final force; command of U.S. joint forces in Europe seems most appropriate for assignment to the Army; and the watch that should be posted on the Asian Main obviously lies within the competence of the Navy.

Organizational changes would achieve little, however, if they failed to represent more basic changes in foreign policy and military strategy.

For U.S. defense forces to be kept strong, they must be kept current. To do that, the United States must keep its imagery true to the reality. The reality of special challenges calls for the imagination to frame special strategies.

Notes

Chapter 1

1. For an exposition of the continuity of the successive administration's policies, see Samuel P. Huntington, "The Defense Policy of the Reagan Administration, 1981–1982," in *The Reagan Presidency: An Early Assessment,* ed. Fred Greenstein (Baltimore: Johns Hopkins University Press, 1983), 82, and especially 84–93.

2. For example, Johnathan Schell, *The Fate of the Earth* (New York: Alfred A. Knopf, 1982); Barbara Tuchman, "The Alternative to Arms Control," *The New York Times Magazine,* 19 April 1982, 44; Robert Lifton and Richard Falk, *Indefensible Weapons* (New York: Basic Books, 1983).

3. See McGeorge Bundy, George F. Kennan, Robert McNamara, and Gerard Smith, "Nuclear Weapons and the Atlantic Alliance," *Foreign Affairs* 60 (Spring 1982):753.

Chapter 2

1. I owe this concept of the liberal vision, and the ensuring precis of its fate, to Robert Gilpin, *U.S. Power and the Multinational Corporation* (New York: Basic Books, 1975), chapter 4.

2. See Daniel Yergin, *Shattered Peace* (Boston: Houghton Mifflin, 1977), especially 263 and following pages.

3. Bernard Brodie, *The Absolute Weapon* (New York: Harcourt, Brace and Company 1946), 50–53, 70–80.

4. Reprinted in entirety in *The New York Times,* 13 January 1954.

5. See Walter Millis, *Arms and the State* (New York: Twentieth Century Fund, 1958), chapter 9.

6. Maxwell Taylor, *The Uncertain Trumpet,* (New York: Harper and Row, 1958), 56–57.

7. "Challenge and Response in United States Policy," *Foreign Affairs* 36 (October 1957):25.

8. See Harold A. Feiveson, "The Dilemma of Theater Nuclear Weapons," *World Politics* 33 (January 1981):282, 285.

9. *The New York Times,* 13 January 1954.

10. U.S. Catholic Conference of Bishops' Pastoral Letter on War and Peace, "The Challenge of Peace: God's Promise and our Response," reprinted in *The Chicago Catholic,* 24 June-19 July 1983, especially 12a–14a; Bundy et al., "Nuclear Weapons and the Atlantic

Alliance;" Richard Ullman, "No First Use of Nuclear Weapons," *Foreign Affairs* 50 (July 1972):669.

11. "Nuclear Strategy," *The Washington Post*, 21 December 1981; "To Buoy Europe's Defenses," *The New York Times*, 10 January 1983.

12. U.S. Congressional Budget Office, *U.S. Ground Forces: Design and Cost Alternatives for NATO and Non-NATO Contingencies* (Washington, D.C.: U.S. Government Printing Office, 1980), xvi, 79–80.

13. Walter Lippmann, *The Cold War* (New York: Harper and Brothers, 1947), 25.

14. Working Group on the Successor Generation, *The Successor Generation* (Washington, D.C.: The Atlantic Council, 1980).

15. See Daniel Boorstin, *The Lost World of Thomas Jefferson* (Boston: Beacon Press, 1948), 228 and following pages.

16. J. Willard Hurst, *Law and the Conditions of Freedom in 19th Century America* (Madison: University of Wisconsin Press, 1956), chapter 1.

17. Ascribed to an (unnamed) "old English judge" in Roosevelt's 1936 Democratic Convention Speech. Aaron Singer, ed., *Campaign Speeches of American Presidential Candidates, 1928–1972* (New York: F. Ungar, 1976), 127.

18. The phrase, "people of plenty," taken from the title of David Potter's book (Chicago: University of Chicago Press, 1954).

19. *1981 U.S. Statistical Abstract* (Washington, D.C.: U.S. Government Printing Office, 1981), 672, 683, 784, assuming that each direct export-related job in manufacturing generates two jobs in indirect production, servicing, and supplies. For a concrete estimate of the dollar and job costs of protectionism in one industry, see Walter Gruzzardi, "How to Foil Protectionism," *Fortune* 107 (March 21, 1983):76, 86.

20. *1981 U.S. Statistical Abstract*, 846–849.

21. Earl C. Ravenal, "The Case for a Withdrawal of Our Forces," *The New York Times Magazine*, 6 March 1983, 58, 60.

Chapter 3

1. See Richard Pipes, "Why the Soviet Union Thinks It Could Fight and Win a Nuclear War," *Commentary*, July 1977, 21.

2. William D. Jackson, "Soviet Images of the U.S. as Nuclear Adversary, 1969–1979," *World Politics* 33 (July 1981):614, 615, and sources cited there.

3. The threat of a Red Army sweep westward quite evidently impressed U.S. planners with its collateral deterrent potential. See

"Strategic Guidance for Industrial Mobilization Planning," in *Containment*, Thomas Etzold and John Gaddis (New York: Columbia University Press, 1978), 302, 303.

4. See George E. Hudson, "Soviet Naval Doctrine and Soviet Politics, 1953–1975," *World Politics* 29 (October 1976):90, especially 107 and following pages; and Michael MccGwire, "Naval Power and Soviet Global Strategy," *International Security* 3 (Winter 1982–83):134, especially 161–167.

5. See Stephen S. Kaplan et al., *The Diplomacy of Power* (Washington, D.C.: Brookings Institute, 1981), chapters 4 and 14; and David D. Finley, "Conventional Arms in Soviet Foreign Policy," *World Politics* 33 (October 1980):1.

6. R. Judson Mitchell, "A New Brezhnev Doctrine: The Restructuring of International Relations," *World Politics* 30 (April 1978):366, 370 and following pages.

7. Robert C. Tucker, "United States–Soviet Cooperation: Incentives and Obstacles," *Annals of the American of Political and Social Science* 372 (July 1967):1, 4–6.

8. George Kennan, "Long Telegram," in *Memoirs, 1925–1950* (Boston: Little, Brown and Company, 1967), 551.

9. See Seyom Brown, "Confronting the Soviet Union: Why, Where, and How?" *Proceedings of the Eighth Annual National Security Affairs Conference,* July 13–15, 1981 (Washington, D.C.: National Defense University Press, 1981), 31, 32–34.

10. See Robert C. Tucker, "Swollen State, Spent Society: Stalin's Legacy to Brezhnev's Russia," *Foreign Affairs* 60 (Winter 1981–82):414.

11. Robert Rothstein, *Global Bargaining: UNCTAD and the Quest for a New International Economic Order* (Princeton: Princeton University Press, 1979).

12. Mitchell, "A New Brezhnev Doctrine," 379 and following pages.

13. Finley, "Conventional Arms in Soviet Foreign Policy," see especially 31.

14. Marshall Goldman, "Will the Soviet Union Be an Autarky in 1984?" *International Security* 3 (Spring 1979):18, 29–36.

15. See Raymond Aaron, "The 1978 Alastair Buchan Memorial Lecture," *Survival* 21 (January-February 1979):2, and especially 3–4.

16. See William Safire's devastating "The Kangaroo Alliance," *The New York Times,* 15 November 1982.

17. Albert Hirschmann, *The Passions and the Interests* (Princeton: Princeton University Press, 1977), 56–66.

18. David Calleo and Benjamin Rowland, *America and the World Political Economy* (Bloomington: University of Indiana Press, 1973), chapter 2.

19. Flora Lewis, "At the Soviet Crossroads," *The New York Times,* 28 September 1982.

Chapter 4

1. McNamara later claimed to have intervened actively against Air Force generals who proposed to take advantage of the temporary U.S. superiority by preparing for a preemptive strike against the Soviet Union. See Robert Scheer, "Interview with McNamara," *The Los Angeles Times,* 8 April 1981.

2. A lucid and concise account by a participant in the SALT I process is Raynond L. Garthoff's "SALT I: An Evaluation," *World Politics* 31 (October 1978):1–5.

3. Ibid., 3.

4. Robert Bathurst, "Two Languages of War," in *Soviet Military Thinking,* ed. D. Leebaert (London: Allen and Unwin, 1981), 32; and see Fritz Ermath, "Contrasts in American and Soviet Strategic Thought," *International Security* 3 (Fall 1978):138, and especially 145–146.

5. The definitions, moreover, were in the tradition of airmen's strategic thought. See Bernard Brodie, *Strategy in the Missile Age* (Princeton: Princeton University Press, 1965), chapters 2 and 3.

6. William W. Kaufmann, *The McNamara Strategy* (New York: Harper and Row, 1964), 47–52.

7. See Harold Brown, *Annual Report to Congress for FY 1982* (Washington, D.C.: U.S. Department of Defense, January 19, 1981), 40–43.

8. William Beecher gave order-of-magnitude figures in *The Boston Globe,* 27 July 1980.

9. See David Gompert's analysis, "Strategic Deterioration," in *Nuclear Weapons and World Politics,* Gompert et al. (New York: McGraw Hill, 1977), 215, 217–221.

10. See James Fallows, *National Defense* (New York: Random House, 1981), 146.

11. One of the most influential and knowledgeable strategic commentators, Richard Garwin, makes the case for this posturing in "Launch Under Attack to Redress Minuteman Vulnerability," *International Security* 4 (Winter 1979–80):117.

12. "A New Approach to Arms Control," *Time* 21 March 1983, 24.

13. Further endorsed, and persuasively defended, by Edmond S. Muskie, "Build Down the Forces We Don't Need," *The Washington Post,* 6 March 1983.

14. William Kaufmann, "The Defense Budget," in *Setting National Priorities: The 1983 Budget,* ed. J. Pechman (Washington, D.C.: Brookings Institute, 1983), 51, 69; Maxwell Taylor, "Build Up the Forces We Really Need," *The Washington Post,* 6 March 1983.

15. John Hackett et al., *The Third World War* (New York: Macmillan, 1978).

16. Rejection of selective central targeting and, by implication, intrawar deterrence is advocated by Spurgeon Kenney and Wolfgang Panofsky, "MAD versus NUTS," *Foreign Affairs* 60 (Winter 1981–82):287, and especially 293 and following pages. See also Michael Howard, "On Fighting a Nuclear War," *International Security* 5 (Spring 1981):7–12, 69, especially the discussion of the views of Colin Gray.

17. See Bruce Bennett and James Foster, "Strategic Retaliation Against the Soviet Homeland," in *Cruise Missiles: Technology, Strategy, Politics,* ed. Richard Betts (Washington, D.C.: Brookings Institute, 1981), 137, 141–142.

18. See Leslie H. Gelb, "The Future of Arms Control: A Glass Half Full," *Foreign Policy* 36 (Fall 1979):21; and Richard Burt, ". . . Or Half Empty," *Foreign Policy* 36:33.

19. See President Reagan's speech on defense, reprinted in its entirety in *The New York Times,* 24 March 1983; see also Michael M. May, *Strategic Arms Technology and Doctrine Under Arms Limitation Agreements,* Research Monograph 37, Center of International Studies (Princeton: Center of International Studies, October 1972), 18–19; and Daniel O. Graham and Gregory A. Fossedal, "A Defense That Defends" and Seymour Weiss, ". . . But Let's Not Overlook the Hurdles," *The Wall Street Journal,* 8 April 1983.

20. As in Richard Ullman's proposal, "U.N.-doing Missiles," *The New York Times,* 28 April 1983.

Chapter 5

1. See the symposium issue, "Germany: Keystone to European Security," *AEI Foreign Policy and Defense Review,"* 4 (March 1983).

2. The term, "protective glacis," is George Kennan's. See his *Memoirs,* 246.

3. Diane Shaver Clemens, *Yalta* (New York: Oxford University Press, 1970), 28 and following pages.

4. See, for example, Dulles's massive retaliation speech, *The New York Times,* 13 January, 1954.

5. See Walter Lippmann, *Isolation and Alliances* (Boston: Little, Brown and Company, 1952), 47–50.

6. Brodie, *The Absolute Weapon.*

7. Bundy et al., *Nuclear Weapons and the Atlantic Alliance,* 757.

8. Elizabeth Pond, "Why Bonn Shudders Over the New Nuclear Debate," *Christian Science Monitor,* 20 April 1982. Nor, needless to say, is retention of the first-use option without U.S. supporters. See, for example, Paul H. Nitze, "A-Arms and NATO," *The New York Times,* 13 April 1982; and Maxwell D. Taylor, "The Trouble with 'No First Use'," *The Washington Post,* 18 April 1982.

9. For example, by McNamara himself, in "No Second Use—Until," *The New York Times,* 2 February 1983.

10. U.S. Congressional Budget Office, *U.S. Ground Forces.*

11. See, in response to Supreme Allied Commander Bernard Rogers's call for all NATO partners to fund a 4 percent defense increase, "West Germany's New Chancellor: The Thoughts of Helmut Kohl," *The Economist,* 18–24 December 1982. General Rogers's views on NATO conventional force needs appeared in "The Atlantic Alliance: Prescriptions for a Difficult Decade," *Foreign Affairs* 60 (Summer 1982):1145.

12. NATO Defense Committee, "Strategic Concept for the Defense of the North Atlantic Area," in *Strategic Guidance,* ed. Etzold and Gaddis, 335, 338.

13. See John B. Bellinger et al. under the supervision of Professor Richard Ullman, *A U.S. Negotiating Position for Nuclear Arms Control in the European Theater,"* Woodrow Wilson School Policy Task Force Report (Princeton: Princeton University Press, January 26, 1981), 28.

14. Pierre Gallois, "The Future of France's Force de Disuasion," *Strategic Review* (Summer 1979):34. And see, for an account of France's increasing reliance in nuclear weaponry, "France's Nuclear Tilt Has NATO Off Balance," *Business Week,* 13 December 1982, 41.

15. Zbigniew Brzezinski, "Reflections on the Crisis in Poland," *Princeton World Review* 1 (Spring 1982):30, 33–34; see, also, Stanley Hoffman, "NATO and Nuclear Wepaons: Reason and Unreason," *Foreign Affairs* 60 (Winter 1981–82), 327, especially 329 and following pages.

16. In Lippmann, *The Cold War,* 46 and following pages.

17. See, for example, James Chace, "Possible West German Neutralism," *The New York Times,* 28 November 1982; Yves Guilliannee, "For France, a Neutralist Germany Is Unacceptable," *The Wall Street Journal,* 26 January 1983; and the political-strategic concerns that pervade Morton Halperin's "Keeping Our Troops in Europe," *The New York Times Magazine,* 17 October 1982, 82.

18. See Flora Lewis, "Alarm Bells in the West," *Foreign Affairs* 60 (1982):551, 557; and Jeffrey Bartwell, "Politics and the Peace Movement in West Germany," *International Security* 7 (Spring 1983):72.

19. Reprinted as "The 1977 Alastair Buchan Memorial Lecture," *Survival* 20 (January-February 1978):3.

20. The Soviet Union's alarm was expressed most pointedly in the proposal worked out by the U.S. and Soviet negotiators at Geneva (Nitze-Kvitsinsky), which called for a Soviet SS-20 cutback and a lower-than-planned U.S. level of deployments, but one that would totally eliminate Pershing II emplacements.

21. Francois de Rose, "Euromissiles' Value," *The New York Times,* 29 March 1983.

22. "The Deployment of Nuclear Weapons," *Atlantic Community Quarterly* 19 (Winter 1981–82):387, 390.

23. See, for example, Francois de Rose, "European Concerns and SALT III," *Survival* 21 (September-October 1979):207; and Lawrence Freedman, "NATO Myths," *Foreign Policy* 45 (Winter 1981–82):48, 53–54.

24. Leslie Gelb, "Soviet Marshall Warns the U.S. on Its Missiles," *The New York Times,* 17 March 1983.

25. Bundy et al., "Nuclear Weapons and the Atlantic Alliance," 757.

26. See, also, "Excerpts from Speech by Andropov on Medium-Range Nuclear Missiles," *The New York Times,* 22 December 1982.

27. "NATO's Nuclear Policy," *The New York Times,* 13 May 1982.

28. Stockholm International Peace Research Institute Brochure, *Armaments or Disarmament* (Salna, Sweden: Bergohamra, 1982), 16.

29. The debate is widely thought to have been touched off by James Fallows's *National Defense,* see especially 39–55.

30. See John J. Mearsheimer, "Maneuver, Mobile Defense, and the NATO Central Front," *International Security* 6 (Winter 1981–82):104.

31. "Improved Conventional Capability for NATO (U)," vol. II, Martin Marietta Aerospace Briefing OA 9432 (Orlando, Fla.: n.d.). For a popularized account, see Deborah Shapley, "The Air-Land Strategy," *The New York Times Magazine,* 28 November 1982, 38.

32. Figures from Barry Blechman and Mark Moore, "A Nuclear Weapon Free Zone in Europe," *Scientific American* 248 (April 1983):37, 39.

33. For example, see, Senator Gary Hart, "What's Wrong with the Military," *The New York Times Magazine,* 4 February 1982, 16.

34. West German "White Paper on Defense," *The Security of the Federal Armed Forces* (Bonn, West Germany: Ministry of Defense, September 4, 1979), 126.

35. See the Boston Study Group, *The Price of Defense* (New York: New York Times, 1979), 117; and John Mearsheimer, "Precision-Guided Munitions and Conventional Deterrence," *Survival* 21 (March-April 1979):68.

36. See Malcolm Hoag's estimates in *Strengthening NATO Capabilities: A "Hi-Lo" Ground Force Mix* (Santa Monica, Calif.: Rand McNally, 1977).

37. Waldo D. Freeman, *NATO Central Region Forward Defense: Correcting the Strategy/Force Mismatch*, National Security Affairs Issue Paper 81-3 (Washington: Natonal Defense University, 1981), 5–7.

Chapter 6

1. See Cyrus Vance, "American Foreign Policy for the Pacific Nations," *International Security* 5 (Winter 1980–81):3.

2. Japanese "White Papers on Defense," excerpted in *Survival* 20 (November-December 1978):264; and *Survival* 22 (January-February 1980):31 and especially 32–34; see also Martin Sours, "Transpacific Interdependencies," in *Region Building in the Pacific,* ed. Gavin Boyd (New York: Pergamon, 1982), 103, and especially 132–35.

3. See Ronald Steel, "With Japan Rearmed," *The New York Times,* 7 December 1982.

4. See Robert Keatley, "Global Slowdown Hits East Asia with Force," *The Wall Street Journal,* 10 January 1983.

5. See Gilpin, *U.S. Power and the Multinational Corporation,* 103 and following pages.

6. See Gerald Garvey, "Foreign Aid Theory: Where Do We Go from Here?" *World Politics* 18 (July 1966):735.

7. For example, Robert Keohane and Joseph Nye, *Power and Interdependence* (Boston: Little, Brown and Company, 1977), especially 27–31.

8. Linkage is discussed in Marvin Kalb and Bernard Kalb, *Kissinger* (Boston: Little, Brown and Company, 1974), 102 and following pages. See, also, Henry Trifomenko, "The Third World and the U.S.-Soviet Competition," *Foreign Affairs* 59 (Summer 1981), 1021.

9. See Steven David, "Realignment in the Horn: The Soviet Advantage," *International Security* 4 (Fall 1979):69, and especially 71–81.

10. See H. Sprout and M. Sprout, *Toward a New Order of Seapower* (Princeton: Princeton University Press, 1946), 14–15.

11. See Alan Henrikson, "The Emanation of Power," *International Security* 6 (Summer 1981):152.

12. As in the massive retaliation speech reprinted in *The New York Times,* 13 January 1954.

13. See Phil Williams, "Whatever Happened to the Mansfield Amendment?," *Survival* 18 (July-August 1976):146.

14. For example, Organization of the Joint Chiefs of Staff, *United States Military Posture for FY 1982* (Washington, D.C.: U.S. Government Printing Office, 1981), 55. See, also, Caspar W. Weinberger, *Annual Report to Congress for Fiscal Year 1983* (Washington, D.C.: U.S. Department of Defense, February 8, 1982), III–103.

15. A break out of unit assignments appears in Jeffrey Record, "The Rapid Deployment Force: Problems, Constraints, and Needs," *Annals of the American Academy of Political and Social Science* 457 (September 1981):109, 117–118.

16. Richard Halloran, "Special U.S. Force for Persian Gulf Is Growing Swiftly," *The New York Times,* 25 October 1982), A14: estimates by the Rapid Deployment Joint Task Force commander, Lieutenant General Robert C. Kingston.

17. Elliott Converse, "U.S. Air Basing Policy, 1945–1950" (Ph.D. diss., Princeton University, 1983), chapter 1, especially 29–31; see also Henry Ladd Smith, *Airways Abroad* (Madison: University of Wisconsin Press, 1950).

18. In Lippmann, *The Cold War,* 21–28.

19. See Stansfield Turner and George Thibault, "Preparing for the Unexpected: The Need for a New Military Strategy," *Foreign Affairs* 61 (Fall 1982):122.

20. See James Cable, *Gunboat Diplomacy: Political Applications of Limited Naval Force* (New York: Praeger, 1971), 134–35.

21. The doctrine is dissected lucidly in Huntington, "The Defense Policy of the Reagan Administration," in *The Reagan Presidency,* ed. Greenstein, 101–104.

22. Sources cited by Huntington, ibid., 111–112.

23. See Jeffrey Record, "A 3-War Strategy?," *The Washington Post,* 22 March 1982.

24. H. Stuart Hughes, "The Second Year of the Cold War," in *The Origins of the Cold War,* ed. Thomas G. Peterson (Lexington, Mass.: D.C. Heath, 1974), 104 and following pages.

25. Robert Komer, "Maritime Strategy vs. Coalition Defense," *Foreign Affairs* 60 (Summer 1982):1124.

Index

About the Author

Gerald Garvey is professor of politics at Princeton University, where he also has served as an editor of *World Politics* and a member of the World Order Studies Committee of the Center of International Studies. Before his appointment to Princeton, he served on the faculty of the U.S. Air Force Academy, on the Air Staff in Washington, and in the offices of the Secretary of the Air Force and the Secretary of Defense. His earlier books are *American Constitutional History* (edited with A.T. Mason, 1965), *Constitutional Bricolage* (1969), *Energy-Ecology-Economy* (1972), *International Resource Flows* (edited with L.A. Garvey, Lexington Books, 1977), and *Nuclear Power and Social Planning* (Lexington Books, 1978).

Center for International Studies: List of Publications

Gabriel A. Almond, *The Appeals of Communism* (Princeton University Press, 1954)

William W. Kaufmann, ed., *Military Policy and National Security* (Princeton University Press, 1956)

Klaus Knorr, *The War Potential of Nations* (Princeton University Press, 1956)

Lucian W. Pye, *Guerrilla Communism in Malaya* (Princeton University Press, 1956)

Bernard C. Cohen, *The Political Process and Foreign Policy: The Making of the Japanese Peace Settlement* (Princeton University Press, 1957)

Myron Weiner, *Party Politics in India: The Development of a Multi-Party System* (Princeton University Press, 1957)

Percy E. Corbett, *Law in Diplomacy* (Princeton University Press, 1959)

Klaus Knorr, ed., *NATO and American Security* (Princeton University Press, 1959)

Rolf Sannwald and Jacques Stohler, *Economic Integration: Theoretical Assumptions and Consequences of European Unification,* trans. Herman Karreman (Princeton University Press, 1959)

Gabriel A. Almond and James S. Coleman, eds., *The Politics of the Developing Areas* (Princeton University Press, 1960)

Herman Kahn, *On Thermonuclear War* (Princeton University Press, 1960)

Robert J.C. Butow, *Tojo and the Coming of the War* (Princeton University Press, 1961)

Klaus Knorr and Sidney Verba, eds., *The International System: Theoretical Essays* (Princeton University Press, 1961)

Glenn H. Snyder, *Deterrence and Defense: Toward a Theory of National Security* (Princeton University Press, 1961)

Sidney Verba, *Small Groups and Political Behavior: A Study of Leadership* (Princeton University Press, 1961)

George Modelski, *A Theory of Foreign Policy* (Praeger, 1962)

Peter Paret and John W. Shy, *Guerrillas in the 1960's* (Praeger, 1962)

Gabriel A. Almond and Sidney Verba, *The Civic Culture: Political Attitudes and Democracy in Five Nations* (Princeton University Press, 1963)

Arthur L. Burns and Nina Heathcote, *Peace-Keeping by United Nations Forces* (Praeger, 1963)

Bernard C. Cohen, *The Press and Foreign Policy* (Princeton University Press, 1963)

Frederick S. Dunn, *Peace-Making and the Settlement with Japan* (Princeton University Press, 1963)

Richard A. Falk, *Law, Morality, and War in the Contemporary World* (Praeger, 1963)

Klaus Knorr and Thornton Read, eds., *Limited Strategic War* (Praeger, 1963)

James N. Rosenau, *National Leadership and Foreign Policy: A Case Study in the Mobilization of Public Support* (Princeton University Press, 1963)

Richard L. Sklar, *Nigerian Political Parties: Power in an Emergent African Nation* (Princeton University Press, 1963)

Cyril E. Black and Thomas P. Thornton, eds., *Communism and Revolution: The Strategic Uses of Political Violence* (Princeton University Press, 1964)

Miriam Camps, *Britain and the European Community 1955–1963* (Princeton University Press, 1964)

Harry Eckstein, ed., *Internal War: Problems and Approaches* (Free Press, 1964)

Peter Paret, *French Revolutionary Warfare from Indochina to Algeria: The Analysis of a Political and Military Doctrine* (Praeger, 1964)

James N. Rosenau, ed., *International Aspects of Civil Strife* (Princeton University Press, 1964)

Thomas P. Thornton, ed., *The Third World in Soviet Perspective: Studies by Soviet Writers on the Developing Areas* (Princeton University Press, 1964)

Richard A. Falk and Richard J. Barnet, eds., *Security in Disarmament* (Princeton University Press, 1965)

Sidney I. Ploss, *Conflict and Decision-Making in Soviet Russia: A Case Study of Agricultural Policy, 1953–1963* (Princeton University Press, 1965)

Harold Sprout and Margaret Sprout, *The Ecological Perspective on Human Affairs, With Special Reference to International Politics* (Princeton University Press, 1965)

Karl von Vorys, *Political Development in Pakistan* (Princeton University Press, 1965)

Cyril E. Black, *The Dynamics of Modernization: A Study in Comparative History* (Harper and Row, 1966)

Harry Eckstein, *Division and Cohesion in Democracy: A Study of Norway* (Princeton University Press, 1966)

Klaus Knorr, *On the Uses of Military Power in the Nuclear Age* (Princeton University Press, 1966)

Center for International Studies: List of Publications

Henry Bienen, *Tanzania: Party Transformation and Economic Development* (Princeton University Press, 1967)

Leon Gordenker, *The U.N. Secretary-General and the Maintenance of Peace* (Columbia University Press, 1967)

Richard F. Hamilton, *Affluence and the French Worker in the Fourth Republic* (Princeton University Press, 1967)

Wolfram F. Hanrieder, *West German Foreign Policy, 1949–1963: International Pressures and Domestic Response* (Stanford University Press, 1967)

Peter Kunstadter, ed., *Southeast Asian Tribes, Minorities, and Nations* Princeton University Press, 1967)

Linda B. Miller, *World Order and Local Disorder: The United Nations and Internal Conflicts* (Princeton University Press, 1967)

James N. Rosenau, ed., *Domestic Sources of Foreign Policy* (Free Press, 1967)

E. Victor Wolfenstein, *The Revolutionary Personality: Lenin, Trotsky, Gandhi* (Princeton University Press, 1967)

Oran R. Young, *The Intermediaries: Third Parties in International Crises* (Princeton University Press, 1967)

William B. Bader, *The United States and the Spread of Nuclear Weapons* (Pegasus, 1968)

Cyril E. Black, Richard A. Falk, Klaus Knorr, and Oran R. Young, *Neutralization and World Politics* (Princeton University Press, 1968)

Richard A. Falk, *Legal Order in a Violent World* (Princeton University Press, 1968)

Robert Gilpin, *France in the Age of the Scientific State* (Princeton University Press, 1968)

Richard H. Ullman, *Britain and the Russian Civil War: November 1918-February 1920* (Princeton University Press, 1968)

Charles De Visscher, *Theory and Reality in Public International Law,* rev. ed., trans. P.E. Corbett (Princeton University Press, 1968)

James Barros, *Betrayal from Within: Joseph Avenol, Secretary-General of the League of Nations, 1933–1940* (Yale University Press, 1969)

Cyril E. Black and Richard A. Falk, eds., *The Future of the International Legal Order,* Vol. I: *Trends and Patterns* (Princeton University Press, 1969)

Ted Robert Gurr, *Why Men Rebel* (Princeton University Press, 1969)

Charles Hermann, *Crises in Foreign Policy: A Simulation Analysis* (Bobbs-Merrill, 1969)

Klaus Knorr and James N. Rosenau, eds., *Contending Approaches to International Politics* (Princeton University Press, 1969)

John T. McAlister, Jr., *Viet Nam: The Origins of Revolution* (Knopf, 1969)

James N. Rosenau, ed., *Kinkage Politics: Essays on the Convergence of National and International Systems* (Free Press, 1969)

Jean Edward Smith, *Germany Beyond the Wall: People, Politics and Prosperity* (Little, Brown and Company, 1969)

Robert C. Tucker, *The Marxian Revolutionary Idea: Essays on Marxist Thought and Its Impact on Radical Movements* (W.W. Norton, 1969)

Harvey Waterman, *Political Change in Contemporary France: The Politics of an Industrial Democracy* (Charles E. Merrill, 1969)

Oran R. Young, *The Politics of Force: Bargaining During International Crises* (Princeton University Press, 1969)

Cyril E. Black and Richard A. Falk, eds., *The Future of the International Legal Orders,* Vol. II: *Wealth and Resources* (Princeton University Press, 1970)

Richard A. Falk, *The Status of Law in International Society* (Princeton University Press, 1970)

Klaus Knorr, *Military Power and Potential* (D.C. Heath, 1970)

John T. McAlister, Jr., and Paul Mus, *The Vietnamese and Their Revolution* (Harper and Row, 1970)

C. Sylvester Whitaker, *The Politics of Tradition: Continuity and Change in Northern Nigeria 1946–1966* (Princeton University Press, 1970)

Cyril E. Black and Richard A. Falk, eds., *The Future of the International Legal Order,* Vol. III: *Conflict Management* (Princeton University Press, 1971)

Francine R. Frankel, *India's Green Revolution: Political Costs of Economic Growth* (Princeton University Press, 1971)

Leon Gordenker, ed., *The United Nations in International Politics* (Princeton University Press, 1971)

Harold Sprout and Margaret Sprout, *Toward a Politics of the Planet Earth* (Van Nostrand Reinhold, 1971)

Cyril E. Black and Richard A. Falk, eds., *The Future of the International Legal Order,* Vol. IV: *The Structure of the International Environment* (Princeton University Press, 1972)

Gerald Garvey, *Energy, Ecology, Economy* (W.W. Norton, 1972)

Anton Bebler, *Military Role in Africa: Dahomey, Ghana, Sierra Leone, and Mali* (Praeger Publishers, 1973)

Klaus Knorr, *Power and Wealth: The Political Economy of International Power* (Basic Books, 1973)

Edward L. Morse, *Foreign Policy and Interdependence in Gaullist France* (Princeton University Press, 1973)

Robert C. Tucker, *Stalin as Revolutionary 1879–1929: A Study in History and Personality* (W.W. Norton, 1973)

Richard Ullman, *The Anglo-Soviet Accord* (Princeton University Press, 1973)

Henry Bienen, *Kenya: The Politics of Participation and Control* (Princeton University Press, 1974)

Ervin Laszlo, *A Strategy for the Future: The Systems Approach to World Order* (Braziller, 1974)

Gregory J. Massell, *The Surrogate Proletariat: Moslem Women and Revolutionary Strategies in Soviet Central Asia, 1919–1929* (Princeton University Press, 1974)

James N. Rosenau, *Citizenship Between Elections: An Inquiry Into the Mobilizable American* (Free Press, 1974)

John R. Vincent, *Nonintervention and International Order* (Princeton University Press, 1974)

Cyril E. Black, Marius B. Jansen, Herbert S. Levine, Marion J. Levy, Jr., Henry Rosovsky, Gilbert Rozman, Henry D. Smith II, and S. Frederick Starr, *The Modernization of Japan and Russia* (Free Press, 1975)

Harry Eckstein and Ted Robert Gurr, *Patterns of Authority: A Structural Basis for Political Inquiry* (John Wiley and Sons, 1975)

Richard A. Falk, *A Global Approach to National Policy* (Harvard University Press, 1975)

Jan H. Kalicki, *The Pattern of Sino-American Crises: Political-Military Interactions in the 1950s* (Cambridge University Press, 1975)

Klaus Knorr, *The Power of Nations: The Political Economy of International Relations* (Basic Books, 1975)

James P. Sewell, *UNESCO and World Politics: Engaging in International Relations* (Princeton University Press, 1975)

Leon Gordenker, *International Aid and National Decisions: Development Programs in Malawi, Tanzania, and Zambia* (Princeton University Press, 1976)

Carl Von Clausewitz, *On War,* ed. and trans. Michael Howard and Peter Paret (Princeton University Press, 1976)

Richard E. Bissell, *Apartheid and International Organizations* (Westview Press, 1977)

David P. Forsythe, *Humanitarian Politics: The International Committee of the Red Cross* (Johns Hopkins University Press, 1977)

Gerald Garvey and Lou Ann Garvey, eds., *International Resource Flows* (D.C. Heath, 1977)

Gerald Garvey, *Nuclear Power and Social Planning: The City of the Second Sun* (D.C. Heath, 1977)

Walter F. Murphy and Joseph Tanenhaus, *Comparative Constitutional Law Cases and Commentaries* (St. Martin's Press, 1977)

Paul E. Sigmund, *The Overthrow of Allende and the Politics of Chile, 1964–1976* (University of Pittsburgh Press, 1977)

Henry S. Bienen, *Armies and Parties in Africa* (Holmes and Meier, 1978)

Harold Sprout and Margaret Sprout, *The Context of Environmental Politics* (The University Press of Kentucky, 1978)

S. Basheer Ahmed, *Nuclear Fuel and Energy Policy,* (D.C. Heath, 1979)

Samuel S. Kim, *China, the United Nations, and World Order* (Princeton University Press, 1979)

James H. Billington, *Fire in the Minds of Men: Origins of the Revolutionary Faith* (Basic Books, 1980)

W.P. Davidson and Leon Gordenker, eds., *Resolving Nationality Conflicts: The Role of Public Opinion Research* (Praeger Publishers, 1980)

Richard A. Falk and Samuel S. Kim, eds., *The War System: An Interdisciplinary Approach* (Westview Press, 1980)

James C. Hsiung and Samuel S. Kim, eds., *China in the Global Community* (Praeger Publishers, 1980)

Robert C. Johansen, *The National Interest and the Human Interest: An Analysis of U.S. Foreign Policy* (Princeton University Press, 1980)

Douglas Kinnard, *The Secretary of Defense* (The University Press of Kentucky, 1980)

Gregory T. Kruglak, *The Politics of United States Decison-Making in United Nations Specialized Agencies: The Case of the International Labor Organization* (University Press of America, 1980)

Bennett Ramberg, *Destruction of Nuclear Energy Facilities in War: The Problem and the Implications* (D.C. Heath, 1980)

Richard Falk, *Human Rights and State Sovereignty* (Holmes and Meier, 1981)

Robert Gilpin, *War and Change in World Politics* (Cambridge University Press, 1981)

James H. Mittelman, *Underdevelopment and the Transition to Socialism: Mozambique and Tanzania* (Academic Press, 1981)

Gilbert Rozman, ed., *The Modernization of China* (The Free Press, 1981)

Robert C. Tucker, *Politics as Leadership,* The Paul Anthony Brick Lectures, Eleventh Series (University of Missouri Press, 1981)

Ali E. Hillal Dessouki, ed., *Islamic Resurgence in the Arab World* (Praeger Publishers, 1982)

Nicholas G. Onuf, ed., *Law-Making in the Global Community* (Carolina Academic Press, 1982)